Of Norwegian Ways

Of Norwegian Ways

By Bent Vanberg

Illustrated by Henning Jensen

Harper & Row, Publishers
New York, Cambridge, Philadelphia, San Francisco
London, Mexico City, São Paulo, Singapore, Sydney

OF NORWEGIAN WAYS. Copyright © 1970 by Dillon Press, Inc. All rights reserved. Printed in the United States of America. No part of this book may be used or reproduced in any manner whatsoever without written permission except in the case of brief quotations embodied in critical articles and reviews. For information address Dillon Press, Inc., 500 South Third Street, Minneapolis, Minnesota 55415. Published simultaneously in Canada by Fitzhenry & Whiteside Limited, Toronto.

First BARNES & NOBLE BOOKS edition published 1984.

Library of Congress Cataloging in Publication Data

Vanberg, Bent.
  Of Norwegian ways.

  Originally published: Minneapolis, Minn.: Dillon Press, 1970.
    1. Norway—Description and travel—1981-
  2. Norway—Social life and customs—20th century.
  I. Title.
DL419.2.V36   1984   948.1'04   83-48396
ISBN 0-06-464078-7 (pbk.)

87 88 10 9 8 7 6 5

Table of Contents

FOREWORD

BEING FOREWORDED IS also, in a way, being forewarned.

As you become, hopefully, better acquainted with Norway, dear reader, you may be in for a few surprises. For instance, out of that country, geographically isolated from the mainstream of ancient and modern cultural and technical developments, came the first patent ever issued for "transmission of pictures, still as well as moving, without the necessity of putting it on film," in short: television. In January, 1924, the Norwegian Patent Board granted this patent to the inventor, Erling Øhrn, who had worked on his idea since 1918. As a designer in a major Norwegian industrial concern he wanted to be able to see the persons he talked with over the phone. Calling his system an "electric eye," he found that it would be ideal for bolstering the security arrangements of his company. Lack of capital and an abundance of skepticism prevented him from continued experiments. Among other Norwegian world's firsts may be mentioned the grenade harpoon for whaling by Svend Foyn in 1873; the modern ski binding with iron lugs (1894); the gas turbine (jet engine), patented in 1884; automatic electrodes for smelting furnaces; hydraulic low pressure winches; blank ammunition of plastics, replacing wooden bullets; and the cheese slicer.

Still another Norwegian first was the ordinary office paper clip. It came about in 1899, and the name of the inventor was Johan Vaaler. Now in use all over the world, this paper clip became a symbol of national unity during the five-year Nazi occupation of Norway in World War II. Loyal Norwegians wore the clip proudly, knowing well that they risked arrest, deportation, imprisonment, and even execution by displaying this simple sign of their true feelings.

Thus, even if Norwegians are not as world famous abroad as they are at home, they are entitled to their pride, which surely the reader will grant them as he proceeds through the pages that follow. There is the story of the Norwegian youngster who moved with his parents to Denmark. When the teacher at his new school asked him where he was born, he at first refused to answer. After considerable prodding he reluctantly told the class: "I just didn't want to brag, but I was born in Norway."

Any foreword, theoretically, should contain a dedication, preferably to one's immediate family, such as one's wife or daughter, "without whose help and understanding this book would have been finished in half the time."

In this case, however, the dedication is to the main subject itself—Norway and its people. And by "its people" is meant all those residing in Norway or outside Norway who proclaim in their hearts—and not only on May 17th—*Jeg ble født i Norge!*" ("I was born in Norway!")

The author's intention has been to open the door to Norway a bit wider in order to provide a spotlight on her sagas, her victories and defeats and on her achievements, which sometimes came slowly, sometimes by leaps and bounds.

As a native Norwegian, this author is a child of the Land of the Midnight Sun. Now, with more than twenty years of residence and citizenship in the United States, he has had the privilege of knowing both the country of his youth and the new land in which he has chosen to live.

In this spirit the book has been written. In this spirit it is hoped it will be received by the reader.

Thank you.

Bent Vanberg

Minneapolis, Minnesota

Look To Norway

LOOK TO NORWAY

DURING World War II when Norway joined the United Nations as one of the Allied powers, President Franklin D. Roosevelt made a speech in which he stated: ". . . if there is anyone who will wonder why the war is being fought, let him look to Norway . . . and if there is anyone who doubts of the democratic will to win, again I say, let him look to Norway. He will find in Norway, at once conquered and unconquerable, the answer to his questioning . . ."

Let us then take a closer look at Norway, the Land of the Midnight Sun — her 3.9 million people, her history, cultural heritage and traditions, industries and trades, political development, her contributions to the world community in almost every field of human endeavor, and her ways of life.

Covering 125,182 square miles—about the size of New Mexico—Norway extends along the western part of the Scandinavian peninsula. One third of the country is north of the Arctic Circle. The North Cape, northernmost point of the European continent, lies as far north as Point Barrow, Alaska, while Lindesnes, the southernmost point is about on the same latitude as Juneau, Alaska. Neighboring nations to the east and northeast are Sweden, Finland and the Soviet Union and to the south, Denmark. Composed of 150,000 islands, out of which only 2,000 are inhabited, the actual length of the country is about 1,000 miles. If one followed the fjord coasts, however, the total distance would stretch to approximately 13,000 miles, or halfway around the world. Of the total Norwegian area, close to 70 percent is rugged mountain expanses, one fourth is forests, 5 percent lakes and rivers, leaving only about 3 percent for cultivation.

Although never a colonial power, Norway nevertheless has something geographically tucked away. After the Vikings retired and eventually disappeared altogether, Norwegians never again went on any land-grabbing rampage abroad. There was an exception in the early 1930's when an attempt was made to secure a slice of Greenland from Denmark. The Danes promptly brought the matter to the International Court in the Hague, Netherlands. The Court almost as promptly chastised the Norwegians in no uncertain terms. In earlier centuries Norway almost always managed to get caught in the feuds between Sweden and Denmark. Whenever Denmark lost a war to Sweden, a part of Norway was generously handed over as an installment on the war reparations. And when the Swedes were put in a similar embarrassing position, they in turn lost no time in offering the victorious Danes a cut of Norway. Norwegian actions of independence in 1814 and 1905 finally brought an end to this method of settling war debts and Norway looked for some possessions of her own. She acquired the Bouvet Island (23 square miles), Peter 1 Island (96 square miles), Jan Mayen (144 square miles), and finally Svalbard (Spitzbergen, with 23,100 square miles), all of which hardly constitute an empire "where the sun never sets," but at least somehow have added to the national pride. Fortunately most of the residents in these "colonies" are polar bears, blue and white foxes, reindeer, musk ox, seals and a few penguins, none of whom seem concerned about their colonial status.

In view of the geographical position of Norway proper, the climate is truly a study in sharp contrasts. First of all, it is much warmer than one would expect. Thanks to the Gulf Stream, sometimes called "the perennial American Marshall Aid," and the general west-east circulation of the atmosphere, the climate is mild and bracing with very little humidity. During the summer, Norway has more daylight than any other country in the world, with no real darkness from the end of April to the middle of August. Thus on Midsummer Day (June 24th) in Hammerfest, the world's northernmost city, there are 24 hours of daylight, while the capital city of Oslo on the same day has 18 hours of sunlight. In addition, Oslo boasts 97 hours more sunshine per annum than Paris and 363 hours more than London. In northern Norway every hotel is equipped with heavy blinds to keep out the sunshine at night. As for temperatures, Norway is warmer than other countries in the same latitude. Precipitation, much of it snow and sleet, is moderate. It is heaviest along the western coast, while the inland areas are comparatively dry. Even Bergen, the largest city on the western coast and known for more rains than any other city, is not actually as bad as this story indicates: An American tourist asked a boy how long it had been raining in Bergen and the boy retorted: "How should I know, sir? I'm only eight years old!" Regional differences notwithstanding, Norway is certainly more solar than polar.

Of 3.9 million Norwegians, about half reside in rural areas and the remainder in cities or smaller towns. The population is mainly concentrated in the coastal districts and in the southeastern valleys. Not surprisingly the population is almost evenly divided, 1,007 women for every 1,000 men. Since World War II, the birth rate has been steady at 17.9 per 1,000. The mortality rate has shown a

marked decline from 15 to 9.9 per 1,000, mainly due to
the considerable reduction in infant mortality. The heavily
reduced emigration to the United States and other over-
seas countries has also substantially influenced the population statistics, while immigration into Norway never has
played any significant role. Norwegians of 40 or more years
of age have a higher life expectancy than any other people,
particularly in the case of women. Life expectancy for
Norwegian men is 71.03, and for women 75.97 years,
while corresponding U. S. figures are 66.4 and 72.7,
Great Britain 68.1 and 73.8, France 62.0 and 71.2, and
Germany 66.7 and 71.7 years.

History Highlights

HISTORY HIGHLIGHTS

THE FIRST SETTLERS of Norway probably came from Central Asia around 10,000 B.C., give or take a few centuries. Unbothered by visas or passports, let alone how many dinosaurs they were allowed to import, they roamed the northern and northeastern parts of the country (now known as Finnmark). Anthropologists and historians have classified these nomads as members of the *Komsa* Culture. From the south — northern Germany through Denmark — came other settlers, today designated as belonging to the *Fosna* Culture, who took up fishing and hunting along the western coast of Norway. The Norway name itself is derived from "Northern way."

The descendants of these early immigrants from Asiatic areas are called Lapps, or Samer, and today they constitute a minority of about 20,000 persons inside the Norwegian border. Altogether the Lapp population is estimated at about 34,000 scattered throughout the northern regions of Norway, Finland, Sweden and the Soviet Union. The Lapps are by no means mainly occupied with reindeer-rearing and tending any more. Most make their living as fishermen and farmers along the coast and inland. They have retained their ancient customs, particularly at weddings, but are otherwise rather modernized in line with the general Norwegian development. They have succeeded, however, in maintaining the unique aspects and expressions of their cultural traditions. A joint Nordic Lapp Council is handling the problems of this minority. In Norway they have their own newspaper, and the State Broadcasting station in the city of Vadsø sends programs in the Samic language.

We do not know for certain when the Norwegians began to explore the seas which washed their shorelines, filled their fjords and brought life to a land long covered by ice. Scientific research states, however, that we have to go all the way back to the Stone Age to find the beginnings of maritime occupations. Findings from that period show that arms and goods for daily use were brought to Norway by ship. Extensive knowledge has been gained concerning the Bronze Age (2,000-500 B.C.). The bronze itself was not produced in Norway but had to be imported, most of it by ship.

Several centuries later, slender and graceful ships with dragon's heads and shield racks carried the Norwegians, now named Vikings (they lived at viker or bays) across the seas. They sailed from their deep, sheltered fjords to raid the shores of England, France and Ireland, bringing riches and slaves back to their farms. Often their fleets of high-prowed vessels, rowed by thirty men or more and displaying colorful striped sails, were veritable armadas. To the people abroad they were a frightening sight. The dragon's heads, gleaming against the rising sun out on the sea, would slowly turn, riding high on the waves and steadily growing in size. Then into view would come the bearded, heavily armed crews, loosening the shields from the racks with the last minute preparations before the ominous attacks.

The Viking art of war was in fact an early version of what during World War II was designated as "amphibian operations." An attack was cleverly timed with the tides, each man knowing exactly his special assignment in order to achieve the well-planned effects. In 844 more than 150 Norse ships entered the river Garonne in France. The following year no less than 800 ships appeared simultaneously outside Hamburg, Germany, and during the Viking siege of Paris in 885 the Norsemen had at least 700 ships at their disposal. London was attacked by approximately 100 ships in the year 994. The Vikings were far more successful in reaching the heart of England than would-be conquerors of more recent times. This fact is pretty well reflected by an anecdote from wartime, Nazi-occupied Norway. A high-ranking German naval officer bellowed heartily at the sight of the three Viking ships on display in Oslo. *"Ach Gott,"* he exclaimed, *"vat iss this. Norwegischer war ships?"* A young Norwegian standing beside him proudly looked up, disdainfully eyeing the Teutonic face and replied calmly: "For your information, *Herr Kapitän,* with these ships we once invaded and conquered England. How did your attempt go?"

One of those vessels on display, the Oseberg ship, was discovered and excavated in the Province of Vestfold in 1903. Though the ship was almost 1,100 years old, it was still possible to steam and bend the planks back to their original shape. Almost all the original materials could be used during the reconstruction. Thus one sleigh was put together from 1,068 fragments, pegs and bolts. The vessel had been the burial ship of Queen Aase, who was pitifully young when she died a thousand years ago. As ruthless, bold and barbaric as the Vikings may have been, they decided to give their queen a royal funeral, wishing her to sail to the womenfolk's *Valhall* in her own yacht, an oak-keeled, dragon-headed, 71-foot-long ship. She was not alone in her burial chamber, which was built like a tent of rough oak planks, partly nailed with iron nails and following the shape of the ship, behind the 43-foot-tall pine mast. An old bond-woman, practically incapacitated by palsy, rheumatism and stiffness of spine (probably the main reason she was chosen to accompany the queen on her last voyage) was also found when the Oseberg ship was unearthed. The skeletons of the two women were still in their richly carved beds, with quilts, pillows and clothing, chests of household goods including scissors and sewing equipment, buckets, dishes and even a wooden pan of surprisingly well preserved apples. Outside the boat remains of twelve horses and six dogs were found. The only animal which apparently had been allowed on board was a peacock. This very rare and valuable bird was entrusted by the Vikings to entertain their beloved queen in tedious moments during the voyage to *Valhall*.

Under King Harald, the grandson of Queen Aase, Norway's history as a nation emerged. He was spurred on by ambition and love for Princess Gyda, who refused to marry him unless he united Norway into one kingdom. Thus Harald met and defeated all his rivals at the sea battle of Hafrsfjord in southwestern Norway in the year 872. Harald was named the "Fair-haired" because he had sworn not to cut his hair before he was the undisputed supreme ruler of a united country. Among succeeding kings, the most significant ones were Olav Tryggvason (995-1000), who introduced Christianity in Norway; Olav Haraldson (1016-1030), who became St. Olav after his death at the battle of Stiklestad; Sverre Sigurdson (1184-1202), who during Norway's most powerful period spoke against Rome and was excommunicated by the Pope; and king Magnus the Law-mender (1274-76), who proclaimed the first codification in the country as a whole.

During the reign of King Magnus Erikson (1319-1355) Norway entered into the first union with Sweden, and following the bubonic plague or the Black Death, which wiped out half of Norway's population, Norway and Denmark became the "twin realms" in a union destined to last almost 400 years. All the kings were Danish, the most notable one being Christian IV, who renamed the capital city of Oslo, Christiania (also spelled Kristiania). This name was kept until 1925 when it was rechristened Oslo, the name originally given the city by King Harald the Hard-Ruler.

The turning point in the Danish-Norwegian relationship came in 1814.

The Norwegian people, who had been subdued for centuries, now secured their constitutional rights under the inspiration of the invigorating ideas of liberty, equality and fraternity from the American and French revolutionaries. The new Constitution, adopted by the National Assembly at the small, idyllic village of Eidsvoll, northeast of Oslo, on May 17, 1814, provided for separate legislative, executive and judicial branches of government. Some of the most important paragraphs incorporated in the Constitution were:

Norway shall be a free, independent, indivisible and inalienable kingdom with a limited and hereditary monarchy as its form of government. Legislative power shall be vested in the 150-member Storting (parliament) to be elected by proportional representation. Executive power, invested in the King, shall be exercised through the Cabinet headed by a Prime Minister, while judiciary power shall be centered in a Supreme Court.

And furthermore:

The King shall always profess the Evangelical Lutheran religion, and maintain and protect the same.

The King may not accept any other Crown or government without the consent of the Storting.

The Representatives shall be exempt from personal arrest

while on their way to and from the Storting, as well as during their stay there, unless they are apprehended for public crimes. Nor shall they be called to account outside the meetings of the Storting for the opinions they have expressed there.

No one may be convicted except according to law, or be punished except according to judicial sentence. Examination by torture must not take place.

There shall be liberty of the Press. Every one shall be free to speak his mind frankly on the administration of the State or on any other subject whatsoever.

No person may be imprisoned without trial.

No law may be given retroactive effect.

The Eidsvoll events had a great impact on the national spirit of pride but complete independence had not yet been attained. A union with Sweden, which seriously strained the relations between the two countries, lasted until June 7, 1905, when Norway broke away. Young Danish Prince Carl was invited to ascend the Norwegian throne and he assumed the name of Haakon VII. This development brought the Danes and Norwegians closer together than at any time during the three centuries of Danish domination. Gradually the Norwegian bitterness toward "big brother" Sweden also subsided. Today the Scandinavians are on the best terms with each other, yet love to poke fun at each other on any given occasion, particularly the Swedes and the Norwegians. Norwegians often find Swedes "stuffy," with too much respect for titles, social position and money. The Swedes, in return, regard Norwegians as "happy-go-lucky" people who are always postponing until tomorrow what they should have done yesterday. They tell about the Norwegian who took a job in a Swedish factory where a sign read: "Coffee break for Swedes — 25 minutes, for Norwegians — 5 minutes." Rather indignant the Norwegian worker asked his boss for an explanation of this kind of discrimination. He was told that "if we gave you Norwegians a longer coffee break, you would have to take a retraining course!" The Norwegians admit freely that the Swedes have the advantage of having a "better neighbor" and the Swedes point out that when a Norwegian goes to his doctor for a check-up and asks the doctor if he will live, the doctor replies that he certainly will live but he would not advise it! The Norwegians will retort that when Swedes pass on, they are usually buried with their heads above the ground because they last longer than any stone! A Norwegian returning from a trip to the United States on board a Norwegian American liner was asked by an American fellow passenger if he was Swedish: "No," he replied, "I'm Norwegian, but I've been terribly seasick!" And as for boasting, the more modest Danes feel that their northern members of the Scandinavian family are about even, with the Norwegians perhaps a bit ahead. The reader may wish to refer to Appendix B for a number of proverbs which might help illuminate the Norwegian character.

The twentieth century brought to Norway complete independence and accommodation with her historical rivals, Sweden and Denmark. Norway was able to remain neutral during World War I. However, the advent of World War II brought forth a new adversary. The crucial test for every single Norwegian character value came on April 9, 1940, when German Nazi forces invaded the country and finally occupied it after two months of military action. The very moment the Norwegian military forces inside the nation had to capitulate, the resistance movement was born. It operated partly underground and partly in the open. Slowly but steadily contact was established with the fighting Norwegian groups outside Norway and communication was centralized through the headquarters of the exiled

Norwegian King and his Government in London, England. Raids and sabotage acts followed. Hitler's henchman in Norway was Vidkun Quisling, leader of the pre-war minority party, Nasjonal Samling. He and his followers were supported by Gestapo terrorists and torturists. Vidkun Quisling had the dubious honor of immortalization through his name. The word "quisling" has come to mean in English, "a person who undermines his own country from within." In spite of executions, deportations and other reprisals, the resistance men and women of Norway contributed substantially to the success of a number of vital sabotage actions. The price paid was often high; yet there was no hesitation shown and many deeds of valor have been recorded to add proof to the fact that the Norwegian people rose to the challenge in a magnificent way.

One particular operation of profound importance and impact comes to mind. This was the daring feat of nine Norwegian resistance fighters who were given the task of destroying a Nazi-controlled "heavy water" plant in the Telemark area to prevent the enemy from perfecting the atomic bomb ahead of the Allies. Their lonely acts of courage succeeded after gliders filled with crack British Commandos had failed and a massive bombing raid by more than a hundred American Flying Fortresses had been unable to knock out the fortress-like factory of Norsk Hydro. Except for these nine brave men, the fate of civilization might have been disastrously different. In key government circles they were credited with altering the course of the war and their story is indeed one of the highly significant achievements which turned the tide for the Allied Forces.

In early 1939 Professor Joliot-Curie of France had advanced so far with his experiments to split the uranium atom that large scale try-outs were possible. He used heavy water as brakes for the chain reaction process and the Norsk Hydro plant at Vemork, Telemark, Norway, was the only heavy water producing site in the world.

In the fall of 1941 the Norwegian underground leaders reported to London that the Germans were showing strong interest in the heavy water producing capacities of Norsk Hydro. It became extremely important to prevent them from making progress in their stepped-up activities in the atomic field, and in July, 1942, the Combined Operations were ordered to destroy the Telemark plant. A famous Norwegian skier, who had managed to escape from the country on a small coastal liner, "Galtesund," captured from the Germans, was sent back to keep London informed. A Norwegian civil engineer had taken photos and made sketches of the Norsk Hydro installations from which a scale model was constructed. Four Norwegian soldiers were sent to Norway to prepare for the arrival of Allied paratroopers ("Operation Swallow"). On November 19, 1942, the group left England but a heavy snow storm prevented jumping. The planes did not have gasoline enough to bring the gliders back to England and the wires were cut. The survivors of the crashed gliders were all killed by the Germans.

Another try was made. Six well-trained Norwegian saboteurs, all top skiers, were dropped on the rugged Hardanger mountain plateau close to the cities of Rjukan and Vemork to join the key members of the underground. They met on February 22, 1943, and a week later the attempt was made. The Germans had reinforced the heavy guard around the Norsk Hydro plant but deemed it impossible for anyone to cross the gap between the two high mountains and to follow the abandoned railroad tracks blasted into the towering mountain side. But the skiers did reach the installation and blew it up as planned.

Their mission completed, the Norwegian saboteurs escaped to Sweden, where they arrived two weeks later, pursued all the way by more than 12,000 German troops and Norwegian quislings.

In August, 1943, the Germans had resumed production of heavy water. Three months later 150 U.S. planes bombed the plant in daylight. The Germans decided to move the remnants of the plant and the finished heavy water to Germany. The Norwegian underground forces were again alerted and managed to place a bomb on board the heavily guarded ferry, which subsequently blew up and was sunk.

Thus Western civilization may have been saved by a handful of Norwegian resistance men who prevented the Nazis from making the atomic bomb ahead of the Allies.

In spite of, or perhaps more correctly as a side-effect of those five long, hard years under the Nazi occupation, the Norwegian sense of humor was very much in evidence. Anecdotes appearing in underground papers and leaflets were relayed throughout the country to brighten an otherwise dreary, terror-filled existence. Anecdotes were told and retold.

In a large department store in Oslo, a German officer came in, approached the young sales lady, clicked his heels, raised his arm and asked: "Heil Hitler! Where is the men's room?" "God save the King, first door to the left!" she replied.

Some Germans stopped a lady in the street, asking for directions. "Do you mind if I answer in English?" she inquired. The soldiers agreed to this, and then she replied, "I don't know," and walked away.

A German officer walked into a restaurant and spotted a man sitting alone at a table. "May I take a seat here?" he asked. The Norwegian did not reply and the officer repeated his request. Still no answer and after the officer had left, the Norwegian was asked rather sharply by a man in the Norwegian quisling uniform, "Didn't you understand what he said?" "Yes," came the retort, "but why should he ask me if he could have a seat after they have grabbed the whole country?"

In 1945, the great year of liberation, one Norwegian sighed and complained how, historically, so much seemed to go against the Norwegians: "In 1814 we lost Denmark, in 1905 we lost Sweden, and now, in 1945 we have lost Germany!"

A Norway Outside Norway

A NORWAY OUTSIDE NORWAY

MORE THAN A THOUSAND YEARS ago the Vikings sailed westward from their Norwegian fjord homes to explore foreign shores. From scattered raids their invasions developed into major expeditions. At times they went southward to France, even penetrating far into the Mediterranean Sea, but mainly their course carried them westward aboard their fast, graceful dragon-headed ships. They settled the Faroe Islands, then discovered Iceland about the middle of the ninth century, spearheading the way for immigrants from Norway. From Iceland they moved on to Greenland where a dominating figure soon emerged. He was Erik the Red, who had left Norway in rather a hurry following some unexplained local killings. His son Leif, later nicknamed the Lucky, was destined to become even more famous. Leif the Lucky was the discoverer of the mainland of North America. To the regions where he landed he gave such names as Helluland or the land of stone slabs, Markland or forest land, and Vinland. Originally it was supposed that *vinland* meant land of wine, but according to more recent scholarly interpretations the word is rather the old Norse term for grassland. These early travels of the Vikings also led to the birth of the first white child in America, a boy called Snorri Thorfinnsson, in the year 1010.

These discoveries around the year 1000 are today historically established facts. They are confirmed by the Norwegian explorer and scientist Dr. Helge Ingstad from the excavations at L'Anse aux Meadows, Newfoundland, and the recently discovered Vinland Map of Yale University, drawn in 1440 and hailed by many scholars as "the most exciting cartographic discovery of the century."

The proper spelling of Leif Erikson's own name is by far a more unsolved issue. There are almost more variations than in chess, from Leif through Leiv, Leifr, Leivr, Leifir and to Eirikson, Eiriksson, Eirikson, Eiricson, Erikson and Ericson, just to present a few samples. One is better off by calling him Leif the Lucky, which was the favorite pet name used by his Norse compatriots. Another quite interesting side issue is the relationship between Old Norwegian Vinlanders and certain American Indians such as the Huron and Iroquois tribes. Linguistic experts indicate that the Indians may have borrowed quite a few words from the Old Norse language. In his book *Lost America,* published in 1950 by Public Affairs Press, Washington, D. C., Arlington H. Mallery points out that words the Indians accepted were applied to the same things as they had covered in Norway. The Norwegian *"ok"* for "and" also became the Indian "ok", *"när"* for "near," *"ata"* for "eat," *"gnista"* for "flame," and *"loki"* for "devil." They all became words among tribal members. The author also adds that this philological fact substantially supports the theory that the Norsemen must have maintained contact with the Indians for quite some time. Modern Norwegian commercial scholars have pointed out that the first commodities of North American foreign trade were handled by the Vikings, who brought furs and ivory from Greenland to Vinland and Markland and traded these items for furs, timber and grapes. They also eagerly accepted maplewood. However, the Viking chieftains vetoed any trade with weapons. Whatever early communication existed between the American aborigines and the Viking visitors, mutual antagonism seems to have eventually developed.

If historically correct, the classic case in point is recorded on the famous and highly controversial runestone of Kensington, Minnesota, which during this century has been the cause of a continuing transatlantic battle among scientists, scholars, runologists, cryptographers and historians. A decisive solution of this riddle seems no closer today than in 1898 when the stone, 36 inches long, 15 inches wide and 5½ inches thick, and weighing 230 pounds was found by the pioneer farmer Olof Ohman under the roots of an 8-inch poplar tree. In runic letters the sad story was found inscribed on the stone. Translations vary substantially, but the following is generally accepted:

"8 Goths and 22 Norwegians on exploration journey from Vinland over the West. We had camp by 2 skerries one days journey north from this stone. We were and fished one day. After we came home (found) 10 red with blood and dead Ave Maria Save from evil." On the edge was written: "Have 10 of our party by the sea to look after our ships 14 days journey from this island Year 1362." Books and articles have been written, lectures held and friendships lost as the question of the validity of the stone and its runic letters has been debated. The runestone now rests in the Museum at Alexandria, Minnesota, where the people proudly proclaim the artifact as "the nation's greatest historical monument," and it will probably be the source of continued controversy for years to come. Whatever the true story, the early Middle Age clashes between the Norsemen and the *skraelings,* as they called the Indians, came to an end when the Vikings returned to Norway. The descendants of the early Norsemen have forgotten neither the Vikings ancestors nor their pets, the elkhounds.

In addition to organizations such as Sons of Norway and Leif Erikson Association, dedicated to a more general recognition of Leif the Lucky Erikson as the true discoverer of America, the elkhound, which often accompanied the Norsemen, also has his Society, The Norwegian Elkhound Association of America. This society honors the Norwegian elkhound as the trail-blazing dog who staked the first tree-claim in the New World.

Long after the Vikings disappeared, Norwegian seafarers continued to find their way to the New World. Captain Albert Andriassen from Halden, Norway, was master of the Dutch vessel "Rensselaerwyck" which came to the port of New Amsterdam, now New York, in 1639. He was the first Norwegian sea captain to enter the harbor. At that time a close commercial friendship existed between the Netherlands and Norway, with hundreds of Norwegians manning the great Dutch fleet. They settled with their families in the new city on the Hudson and Norwegian girls married into the Vanderbilt, Schuyler, Stuyvesant, Van Cortlandt and Van Rensselaer families. A Norwegian served as the interpreter when Manhattan Island was sold by the Indians for $24.

In his work *The History of the George Washington Family* Albert Wells traces Washington's ancestry back to the Norwegian Earl Haraldson. Washington was an honorary member of the first Scandinavian society in America, "Societas Scandinaviensis," organized in Philadelphia in 1769. Its first president was Captain Abraham Markoe, a Norwegian-French Huguenot. A year later the Society held a banquet commemorating the recognition of the United States of America by the Scandinavian countries.

There have been modern-day Vikings like Fridtjof Nansen (1861-1930), who in 1888 crossed the Greenland ice cap on skis and brought his ship "Fram" closer to the North

Pole than any vessel ever had been. Later he became a great scientist, statesman and humanitarian. Roald Amundsen (1872-1928) on December 11, 1911, was the first to reach the South Pole and plant the Norwegian flag. In 1903-06, he was the first navigator to take a ship through the Northwest Passage from east to west. The ship "Gjøa" is today located in San Francisco. In recent years Thor Heyerdahl (1914-   ) drifted 101 days with his Kon-Tiki raft from Ecuador to Polynesia to prove that there exists the possibility of a sub-stratum of American Indian culture in these Pacific islands. In 1970 he crossed the Atlantic from Egypt in a "paper boat," the "Ra II."

The Norway of the 19th century was a nation undergoing rapid change, which often meant dislocation and upheaval. A significant dimension was added to the political, theological, economic and cultural struggles: The Emigration to America.

Whether from a national, social or ordinary human point of view, no other factor has played such an important part as this large-scale migration. The man behind it all was Cleng Peerson.

He was a leader of men but a lonely man. As a realist and a dreamer he was a study in contrasts. Those who shared his visions blessed him while he was condemned by others who termed him a seducer of a whole people and a traitor to his own country. He founded a Norway outside Norway and became the "Father of Emigration."

He was born May 17, 1782 at Tysvaer, near Haugesund, Western Norway. However, surprisingly little is known about his innermost thoughts, ideals and guiding principles. What we do know is sufficient to form a rather clear impression of a farmer's son who educated himself through travel to many lands. Cleng Peerson was destined to lead an exodus that laid the foundation for a new concept of the Norwegian in America.

The westward wave of emigrating Norwegians started in the wake of a 30 ton, 45 foot sloop, the "Restauration," which left the city of Stavanger with 45 passengers and a seven man crew on July 4, 1825, and arrived in New York on October 9th. On the journey the passenger list had increased with the addition of a baby girl. All were looking for the same thing—a new existence in a new world. They were met at the pier by Cleng, who himself had first seen America, "the land of milk and honey," as he called it, four years earlier. He calmed their uneasiness, restored their spirit and regained their confidence which had ebbed during those long months at sea. Cleng Peerson would become a legend in his own lifetime. Spurred by his inherent restlessness and urge to find a constantly improved life for his fellow countrymen, he was always on the go. He was a true optimist who took the cold water thrown on his ideas, heated it with his own enthusiasm, made steam and pushed ahead. At Norse, Bosque County, Texas, he found his final resting place, and died on December 16, 1865.

From 1825 to 1900 more than 850,000 Norwegians left their homes and country to make a new life for themselves and their families in the United States and Canada. They gained dignity and stature as they were assimilated by their new strange surroundings. Their contributions to the growth and development of their adopted country have been amply acknowledged by historians and hailed by many of non-Norwegian descent:

President Abraham Lincoln: ". . . I know the Norwegians from Illinois, and I know that no immigrants have advanced America more than they . . ."

President Calvin Coolidge: (at the Minneapolis, Minnesota ceremonies commemorating the Norwegian Emigration Centennial in 1925): ". . . When I see you and think of what you are and what you have accomplished, I know that the future of our country is secure in your hands. You have given your pledge to the Land of Freedom—and the pledge of the Norwegian people has never yet gone unredeemed . . ."

Governor Adlai E. Stevenson: ". . . The story of Norwegian settlement in the United States is rich in human interest and historic significance, withal, it is a peaceful drama in which patience, courage, thrift and hard endeavor find fitting economic, political and cultural rewards. . . . Throughout our republic, the well-knit fabric of American society is far more colorful and immeasurably stronger by reason of the strong strands woven into it by men and women of Norwegian blood . . ."

Some of the immigrants and their sons and daughters gained nationwide fame through their efforts to promote the material, social and spiritual welfare of their communities. Others stuck quietly to their daily chores, but they all helped lift their part of the country to new economic and cultural heights through their Norwegian heritage.

They all exemplified a certain transplanted stubbornness to promote and to prosper. Tens of thousands stayed in New York and other Eastern states, while the vast expanses of the Middle West became the final destination for large groups.

Others who arrived on these shores lifted their heads and sensed that something was lacking, something they knew was indispensable in order to round out their new existence. They drove, rode and marched across the endless prairies, the lonely deserts and the majestic mountains, beyond which another vast ocean and giant trees were waiting for more manpower. To them this was Norway all over again, but on a far greater scale. For them this was the ultimate destiny. Out of these new strange surroundings the sturdy Norwegian settlers carved their livelihood, molded their future and enriched their own lives. The sons and daughters of these courageous pioneers braved hardship and danger during the transitional period and proved themselves worthy of the task to guard, preserve and expand their heritage.

The extent of the emigration from Norway to the United States differed slightly according to good or bad times in the Old Country. These are the main figures:

1820-1830	94
1831-1840	1,201
1841-1850	13,903
1851-1860	20,931
1861-1870	71,631
1871-1880	95,323
1881-1890	176,586
1891-1900	395,323
1901-1914	224,541
1915-1922	30,277
1923-1930	52,655

From the beginning the Norwegians in the New World not only enjoyed the advantages of their adopted country, but also responded to calls for her defense. A number of seamen served in the colonial army in New York; others served under John Paul Jones during the Revolutionary War.

Many Norwegian pioneers also became engaged in the Civil War through the formation of the 15th Wisconsin Volunteer Infantry Regiment in February, 1862, under the young Norwegian officer, Hans C. Heg. He exhorted his compatriots in the Norwegian language paper *Emigranten,* published in Madison, Wis. ". . . Countrymen! Almost before we know it, we are plunged into the midst of the most significant war that has ever been waged in any land. The rebels have not permitted themselves to hold back because of the patience and forbearance of the Union. . . . There is no question of party power or principle. It is the Country's safety, preservation of our popular form of government, preservation of our civic and religious freedom and, in consequence, also our temporal welfare is at stake. . . . The government of our adopted country is in danger. That which we learned to love as free men in our old Fatherland . . . our freedom, our government, our independence . . . is threatened with destruction. . . . Shall we Scandinavians sit still and watch our American, German and English-born fellow citizens fight for us without going to their aid? Come then, young Norsemen, and take part in the defense of our country's cause . . . Let us band together and deliver untarnished to posterity the old and honorable name of Norsemen . . ."

Although the regiment was called "The Scandinavian Regiment," it was preponderantly Norwegian and it was organized on the promise that it would be led by a Norwegian and that Norwegian would be its language. The regimental flag was presented to the group by the Nora Lodge, a Norwegian society in Chicago, and is now displayed at the Norwegian-American Museum in Decorah, Iowa. It carries American and Norwegian emblems and the inscription in Norwegian, *"For Gud og Vort Land"* ("For God and our Country"). The 15th consisted of about 850 men and suffered considerable losses in various battles. Colonel Heg fell at Chickamauga, Georgia, in September, 1863. The various companies with rousing names such as The St. Olaf Rifles, The Wergeland Guards, Odin's Rifles and The Norway Bearhunters were mustered out in February, 1865.

Norway was neutral during World War I although

heavy losses were inflicted on her merchant marine by German U-Boats. When Norway was attacked and occupied by the Nazi forces in 1940, the aroused Norwegian-American communities rallied to her help, mainly through drives coordinated by "American Relief for Norway," a nationwide organization. Close to $32,000,000 in cash and goods was contributed through these efforts. Similar actions in Canada raised more than $650,000.

Militarily, the Norwegians in America again created their "own" unique unit, this time a battalion of volunteers who were of Norwegian extraction and had a working knowledge of the Norwegian language. In addition they had to be good skiers. Under provisions of a War Department Letter, the 99th Infantry Battalion (Spec.) U.S. Army was activated on July 10, 1942, at Camp Ripley, Minnesota. The purpose of the 99th was to utilize the special skills of its members in the event of an Allied invasion of Norway. Every one of the one thousand men was required to take part in the Norwegian language courses but soon the students were teaching the imported tutors. The result was that nearly 60 percent were excused from the language classes. Following extensive training at Fort Snelling, Minnesota, Camp Hale, Colorado, and Camp Shanks, New York, the battalion was sent to Great Britain and saw action in France, Belgium, and Germany. Then on to Norway for the fulfillment of the original assignment: to help the Norwegian forces, who for the first time saw the Viking ship emblem carried on the strong Norwegian-American shoulders. In recognition of its service, the 99th, which was battle-scarred from the European war fields, had the special honor of parading for H. M. King Haakon VII when the monarch returned to free Norwegian soil.

During World War II three figures emerged from the

Norwegian-American military ranks: Brigadier General Lauris Norstad, Major General Leif Sverdrup, and Colonel Bernt Balchen.

General Norstad was born in Minneapolis, Minnesota in 1907 and raised in Red Wing, Minnesota. He was graduated from the U. S. Military Academy in 1930. In 1947 he became the Deputy Chief of Staff for Operations of the U. S. Air Force and in 1956 Supreme Allied Commander in Europe (SACEUR). General Norstad retired from active service in 1963. Among numerous orders he holds the Grand Cross of the Royal Norwegian Order of St. Olav.

Major General Leif Johan Sverdrup was born at Bergen, Norway in 1898. Like Norstad, he was the son of a minister. At age seventeen he came to America, became an engineer and established his own consulting engineering company in St. Louis. During World War II he built airfields in the southwest Pacific area and rose to the rank of Major General, commanding 110,000 men. He became a close friend of General MacArthur and was on board the battleship "Missouri" during the Japanese surrender. Sverdrup once wrote: ". . . To one who has chosen, as an immigrant, to seek adoption by the United States of America, the opportunities and freedoms remain perpetually in sharp focus. . . . Why are the freedoms which I enjoy as a citizen of the United States etched so indelibly on my consciousness—and in my heart? . . It is simply that the liberty which you and I enjoy here is not and never has been matched so completely by any other country in the world. . . . To all who will reach out after it, life in the United States is as varied and exciting as it is replete with opportunities . . ." He is Commander of the Royal Norwegian Order of St. Olav.

Bernt Balchen was born at Tveit, Norway, in 1899. He

won his initial fame as an aviator and explorer. In 1927 he piloted the Fokker Tri-Motor America on a nonstop flight across the Atlantic and two years later piloted the first flight over the South Pole. Earlier he had helped the Norwegian explorer Roald Amundsen and the American Admiral Richard E. Byrd on their epic flights to the North Pole.

During World War II he became famous for his air-rescue work over the vast Greenland tracts and as supervisor of the air evacuation—in unmarked planes—of some five thousand Allied airmen interned in Sweden. He also conceived the plan and laid the groundwork for the U. S. Air Force's huge base at Thule, Greenland. Bernt Balchen was the first person since Lafayette to become a United States citizen by special Act of Congress. He has become an almost legendary character. In addition to being an expert on polar strategy he is author of a cook book and recognized as an outstanding watercolorist. He holds the rank of Commander First Class with Swords and Stars, of the Royal Norwegian Order of St. Olav.

In Appendix A the reader will find a Who's Who of Norwegians and Americans who were born in Norway.

From Stave to State Church

FROM STAVE TO STATE CHURCH

WHEN THE Viking kings introduced Christianity into Norway in the middle of the 10th century, they did it with the same zest and methods as they used on their exploits abroad. Going from valley to valley they forcefully convinced stubborn skeptics that the days of the old gods were numbered. To really bring home their point they tore down the *hov,* the building dedicated to the gods and smashed all wooden images. Undoubtedly the people were surprised that the powerful chief god Odin or his strong aide Tor with the magic hammer *Mjølner,* which always returned to his hand, did not retaliate at all. Yet many were reluctant to give up the array of colorful gods that had ruled their lives and fates from their headquarters in *Asgard* with *Valhall* (the hall of the Fallen Warriors) as the main residence.

All Vikings who had fallen in battles on earth were said to have had a marvelous time in *Valhall.* All day they fought against each other out on the plain and in the evening *Odin* gathered them all, living or dead, to a party where they were entertained by *Odin's* maidens, the *Valkyries.* The *Valkyries* were young and beautiful and they rode in full armor all over the world to handpick those Vikings whom they wanted to take with them to Valhall. It is said that the ancient Colosseum in Rome possibly inspired the Vikings' concept of *Valhall.* The structure, seating 100,000 and with 520 doors and nearly a mile in

circumference had made an enormous impression on the
Norsemen and tempted them to give the *Valhall* of their
gods similar dimensions.

In addition to *Odin* and *Tor* there were such gods as
the kind and saintly *Balder;* the brave *Ty;* the watchman
Heimdall with his *Gjallarhorn* that could be heard around
the world; the silent *Vidar; Aege,* the god of the seas; *Ullr,*
the god of skiing; and *Njord,* the god of the winds and the
fire. Then there was *Frey* who ruled over rain, sunshine
and the harvests and who brought prosperity and happiness to men and sorrow to no one. The only bad god was
Loki, who managed to create quite a few difficulties for
his fellow-gods but nevertheless was tolerated as one of
them. As for the goddesses, the top ranking was of course
Odin's wife *Frigg,* followed by the goddess of love, *Freya.*
Others were *Vaar,* the goddess of fidelity; the virgin *Gev-
jon;* and *Nanna,* the wife of the good god *Balder.* Her
heart broke when he was killed by the evil *Loki.*

The influence of the gods diminished as the young Norwegian Christian church gained ground and came under
strong English influence. The first church built was dedicated by King Olav Trygvasson (995-1000) and one may
still see and admire several characteristic stave-churches
dating back to the 11th and 12th centuries. The origin of
the stave church is a controversial issue. Some historians
believe it was rooted in the heathen cult of the Viking
Age and the frequent use of dragons' heads and serpent
ornaments seems to support the theory. Others say that the
stave church represents the Norseman's adoption of the
Gothic-style church. The stave churches may well be the
works of ship's carpenters. The method of locking the
heavy planks together and the use of knees at supporting
joints seems to show this. The carved dragons' heads, so
similar to those found on the prows of Viking ships, are

mounted on many of the cornice peaks and may be another influence of the ship builder.

Very little is known about the history and the cultural background of the stave churches, and it is only recently that historians and archeologists have taken an active interest in finding out more about them. Interesting research work is being done in the stave churches of Norway. There were more than 750 of them in Norway during the Middle Ages but only 25 remain today. Some were burned down, some were wantonly destroyed through vandalism and many were torn down in order to make room for more modern edifices. An exact replica of the most famous of all stave churches, the Borgund Church in Western Norway, is now to be found at Canyon Lake, Rapid City, South Dakota. It is called "The Chapel in the Hills" and has become a major tourist attraction in the Black Hills area as well as the home of the Lutheran Vespers, the Radio Voice of the Commission on Evangelism of the American Lutheran Church. In the first year after its completion, the Rapid City replica was visited by more people than have visited the original Borgund Church during the past 800 years.

The Lutheran Reformation was introduced in Norway in 1537. It marked a shift from English to German influence that remained down to our times. However, new impulses have come from England and the United States through dissident movements and splinter churches. Possibly the most significant movement in the history of Christianity in Norway was the one instigated by the farmer's son Hans Nielsen Hauge, born in 1771. Of a strongly religious character, Hauge underwent a profound spiritual rebirth in 1796 and for the next eight years preached in many parts of Norway, distributing his own books and pamphlets. He was imprisoned a number of times but the attempts by the authorities to stop him were in vain. His longest jail term lasted ten years when he was heavily fined and finally released in 1824. He never tried to form an independent society of the groups of "Hauge friends." He advocated strongly that they should remain in the State Church. Though Hauge died in 1824, the effect of his movement became increasingly felt, even in public life where the common people felt they had been unfairly treated. Important reformative laws were passed by the Parliament.

Among the passengers on board the sloop "Restauration," which spearheaded the modern emigration from Norway to the United States, were several members of the Hauge movement. The most prominent of these was Ole Olsen Hetletvedt, the father of the Norwegian church in America. Another powerful spokesman for the Haugean movement was Elling Eielsen, who linked the Norwegian settlers of Illinois, Wisconsin and other midwestern states.

Today the Norwegian State Church includes more than 96 percent of the total population. It is divided into ten dioceses and close to six hundred parishes, served by some one thousand clergymen with salaries fixed by law, making the pastors financially independent of their congregations. Church services such as baptisms, confirmations, weddings and funerals are free of charge.

According to the most recent statistics, non-members of the State Church constitute about 3¾ percent of the population, most of them belonging to the Norwegian Pentecost Congregations, The Free Evangelical Lutheran Church, the Methodists, the Baptists, the Roman Catholics, Greek Catholics, the Adventists, the Norwegian Missionary Congregations, the Jehovah Witnesses, Anglicans, the Mormons and the Orthodox Jews. The ban against Jews, which was included in the 1814 Constitution and barred them from entering Norway, was abolished in 1831; twenty years later the first Jews arrived from Russia. The first Jewish Society was organized in Oslo in 1892 and the Jewish population increased to some one thousand four hundred persons in 1941. During the Nazi occupation almost half of them were arrested and sent to concentration camps in Germany. Of these only thirteen survived. Immediately after the liberation in 1945, all civil rights were restored for the Jews, all confiscated property returned to the lawful owners and a resettlement program for displaced persons initiated. The government authorized the admission of several hundred displaced persons into Norway and the Norwegian people swiftly followed up by providing free transportation, housing, equal civil rights and full benefits of the Norwegian social services. The displaced persons were able to become citizens in five instead of the normally set ten years.

Following World War II some hundred and fifty new churches were built to replace those bombed or burned out during the occupation years.

According to the primate of Norway, Bishop Fridtjov Birkeli of Oslo, more than four hundred new congregations are needed in Norway before the end of this century to accommodate population shifts.

The possibility of separating church and state has been discussed for years in Norway. The bishop doubts, however, that a majority of the political leaders would favor such a move. Other church leaders disagree.

Maintenance and operation of home and foreign missions are provided through close cooperation between the State Church and a substantial number of societies supported by voluntary contributions from members. In one recent year these contributions amounted to about $16 million. Foreign missionary work began in the early

1700's in Greenland. In 1842 the Norwegian Missionary Society was formed and is now supported by a total
income of $3.5 million annually. More than one thousand
Norwegian missionaries are now at work in over thirty
countries. The Norwegian Church belongs both to the
World Council of Churches and the Lutheran World Federation.

"Fram, Fram Kristmenn, Krossmenn"

"FRAM, FRAM KRISTMENN, KROSSMENN"

COMPULSORY education in Norway dates back to 1827, the year the Primary School Act was passed. Since 1889, school attendance has been compulsory at the primary level lasting seven years. All normal children are required to start school the year in which they reach the age of seven. It is characteristic of the Norwegian school system that each type of school has special legislation relating to it. Local authorities are now experimenting with an additional two years of compulsory schooling aimed at achieving the greatest possible degree of equality in educational opportunity.

The extension of compulsory education involves the amalgamation of two types of secondary schools — the *realskole* and the *framhaldsskole*—to form a further stage in the primary school. This experimental nine-year school is organized either as a six-year elementary school (*barneskole*) and a three-year secondary school (*ungdomsskole*), or as a seven-year elementary school and a two-year secondary school. Most schools are now of the six plus three type. A few municipalities, mainly in sparsely populated districts, are testing the seven plus two pattern.

The basic subjects taught in the traditional seven-year school include Norwegian language, home environment, history, geography, natural science, arithmetic, writing, art, music, handicrafts, physical education, English and

religion. (Children of parents committed to a religious
faith other than that of the Norwegian State Church are
excused from the religious instruction). The final examination for seventh graders includes written tests in Norwegian, arithmetic and sometimes English. American
pedagogues who have made studies of the Norwegian educational system have stated that "the fine teaching accomplished in foreign languages is evidenced by the compe-
tency displayed even by seventh graders after only two years
of English and by the graduates of the English sequence in
the secondary schools. The quality of their pronunciation,
vocabulary, and grammar appears from observation and
experience to be unusually good, and if the same standards
are met for other languages, as indeed they no doubt are,
this aspect of Norwegian education is certainly achieving the aim of functional use outside of school of that
which has been learned in school." The same observers
note that problems of teacher education in Norway sound
familiar to those who are struggling with similar difficulties in the United States. Such questions as the amount
of professional education needed, the relation between theory and practice, and the types and quality of student
teaching apparently are international. "But most hearten-
ing of all," they conclude, "is perhaps the very high
respect accorded teachers in Norway, both professionally
and socially. They are a dedicated group and deserve the
prestige they have attained. Their contribution to the society as a whole cannot be minimized, and some credit for
the country's progress in politics, government, and social
welfare must be given to the quality of education attained
by the average worker as well as the high level attained by
the leaders. Certainly the Norwegians can point with pride
to their educational institutions and to the people who are
responsible for them."

In their eighth year, students have some choice in subjects, according to their ambitions and interests. In the ninth year instruction is as a rule modified according to whether the student wishes to emphasize Norwegian, mathematics, English or German. Students are also allowed to choose certain subjects in addition to the obligatory course of studies. The combination of academic studies that leads to the three year *gymnas* requires study of two foreign languages, English and German. Other courses are partly academic and partly practical.

The school system is almost entirely public supported. The cost of higher education and research is borne wholly by the state. The academic school year usually covers thirty-eight weeks, with six school days in each week. Experiments have, however, been conducted concerning Saturday as a day without school. The normal timetable for most school children contains thirty-six forty-five minute periods per week. There are also special schools for handicapped children.

The educational structure of Norway also includes two state-financed universities and five university colleges. The University of Oslo was founded in 1811 and started its activities two years later, while the University of Bergen was established in 1946. The State Institute of Technology, located in Trondheim, functions in accordance with a special Act of 1936. The other State Colleges are for Teachers, Business Administration and Economics, Agriculture, and Theology.

There are various summer schools and seminars, courses and institutes offering classes in Norwegian culture and language. The best known and recognized is the University of Oslo International Summer School. Started in 1947 as the Summer School for American Students and aimed at the academic youth of the United States and

Canada, the School soon received students from other nations as well. To date students and scholars from more than seventy countries have participated. Based on the idea that Norway and its cultural contributions have a genuine quality which makes studying them a valuable experience, the scope of the School has been gradually widened. In addition to the core of the curriculum, a General Survey of Norwegian Life and Culture, elective courses are offered in many specialized subjects. All participants take examinations and those who pass receive the University's Summer School Certificate of Achievement. More than eight thousand students from the United States over the years have attended the Summer School and have been able to transfer credits to their home universities or colleges since all courses are set up in terms of North American semester hours.

The summer stay in Norway has also been highlighted by various excursions throughout the country. The gathering of many nationalities in the friendly, constructive atmosphere of a small north European country provides a highly stimulating intellectual milieu. A considerable number of scholarships are available in Norway as well as in the United States, where the Summer School office is located at St. Olaf College, Northfield, Minnesota.

Other institutions in Norway provide training in all practical and technical fields such as handicrafts and industry, housekeeping, commercial and clerical education, navigation, marine engineering, fishing, horticulture, forestry, dairy schools, nursing, midwifery, library science, journalism, hotel management, theater, arts, railroads, postal and telegraph services, customs, mining, etc.

The Folk High Schools aim at providing adult youth continued general education. Based on the fundamental ideas set forth by the Danish pastor and poet J. F. S.

Grundtvig, the first Nordic Folk High School was opened in 1844 in Denmark; Herman Anker and Ole Arvesen started the first in Norway in 1864. Several more were founded and particularly at the turn of the century these schools flourished as important cornerstones in the overall educational program. At the beginning the main objective was to promote democratic ideals and educate the students for an active democratic life, but now practical subjects have become more prominent in the curriculum.

By a law enacted in 1949 the Folk High Schools are now joined to the Province Schools and the private Youth Schools. Most of the students still come from the rural districts, but some of these schools now also attract participants from urban and suburban areas.

A recent study of school children in the United States, Great Britain, France and Norway yielded some interesting comparisons. In Norway about 90 percent of the children rise when the teacher enters the classroom, and in the U. S. only 19 percent. Norwegian children are more active after school hours than youngsters in the other countries, mainly because they quit earlier in the afternoon. Norwegian parents are apt to let their children have more freedom Friday and Saturday nights. The strictest parents in this respect are found in France and Great Britain. In Norway the children make more use of the classrooms after school hours than in the other countries. They see more movies, mainly because television is by and large still in its infancy.

As for church attendance, American and French children are in the lead. In Norway only 19 percent of the children are in church on Sunday. American children are more willing helpers at home, but, like Norwegian children, they get paid for it. In outdoor activities and book reading, the Norwegian children are ahead of the others.

More than 40 percent of Norwegian homes have at least one hundred volumes on their shelves, compared with 27 percent of American homes. Current events are most frequently discussed at French dinner tables, followed by Norway, United States, and England. American and Norwegian children use the telephone most, French children the least and most conversations last fifteen minutes. To test the knowledge of the children in all these countries they were asked questions of a general nature such as: Who was Mozart? What is the speed of light? Where is the Amazon River? How much is 30 percent of 50? The British children provided the most correct answers, followed by the German, Norwegian, French and American students. Respect for the teacher is more evident in Norway and France, least in the United States. Curiously enough there were more American children who stated that they wanted to become teachers. Asked if they preferred to be more popular among their school friends than to be the best in the class, most Norwegian children preferred top grades. The same was true for the children in the other countries, except France. In summer studies the Norwegian children had the least interest.

Physical education in Norway is organized by the State Office for Sport and Youth, a section of the Ministry of Church and Education. Gymnastics, sports and games are taught in every school. The State College of Physical Education is located in Oslo and specializes in physical education and recreation for schools, the armed forces and sports clubs.

Most of the Norwegian sports clubs are affiliated with the national Sports Federation.

Physical activity and health with special emphasis on the needs of handicapped persons have become a matter of prime concern to physical educators and physicians during recent years. A special Health Sports Center to be located at Valdres is projected, and to stimulate interest in it, annual ski races for blind persons have been staged with the motto: "Learn to See with Your Thoughts."

The education of their children was the prime concern and ambition of the pioneering Norwegians in America though they themselves were completely engaged in the struggle to secure a livelihood for their families. These ambitions and aspirations manifested themselves in colleges which today rank among the finest in the country.

Luther College in Decorah, Iowa, is the oldest college founded by people of Norwegian descent. Established in 1861 in La Crosse, Wisconsin, the college moved the following year to Decorah, the site which originally had been chosen. In 1936 the college became coeducational and now has more than two thousand students and ninety faculty members. For a number of years Luther College has conducted an Institute in American Studies for Scandinavian Teachers in English, predominantly attended by Norwegian pedagogues.

For ninety years the College has also owned and maintained the official Norwegian-American Museum, located in downtown Decorah. It was opened in 1877 and is believed to be the Museum which best depicts the history of a nationality. It was the first institution of its kind created by an ethnic group in America for the purpose of preserving its history and cultural heritage. Its first display was a collection of birds' eggs, including specimens representative of Scandinavian birds. Since 1964 it has been operated as an independent non-profit corporation and now is a repository for artifacts illustrating the life of the Norwegian immigrant both before he left his native country and after he settled in America.

St. Olaf College in Northfield, Minnesota, was founded

as an academy in 1874 by a group of pioneers, pastors and businessmen. In 1886 a college department was added. Throughout its history the college, which now includes about two thousand five hundred students and a faculty of about one hundred fifty, has been closely related to The American Lutheran Church. For a number of years the head of the Norwegian department at St. Olaf was Ole Edvart Rolvaag (1876-1931), author of the epic *Giants in the Earth — A Saga of the Prairie,* which is dedicated to "Those of my people who took part in the great settling, to them and their generations."

St. Olaf College has its Norwegian motto *"Fram Fram Kristmenn Krossmen"* ("Forward, Forward, Christians, Crusaders") and other strong accents of its Norwegian background.

St. Olaf is the home of the Norwegian American Historical Association, which was organized October 6, 1925, just one hundred years after the arrival of the first immigration vessel, the "Restauration." In 1926 it was incorporated by a group of far-sighted, historically minded Norwegian-Americans with the avowed purpose of recording the history of the Norwegian people who emigrated to the United States. It was their plan that this history should chronicle the contributions of the Norwegian immigrants and their descendants to the development of this country. In fulfillment of this purpose the Association has published about fifty books, promoted Norwegian-American historical research and literary works, and helped to maintain and develop archives of Norwegian-American historical material.

Augsburg College, originally located at Marshall, Wisconsin, was the first theological school founded by Norwegian Lutherans in America. Later it was expanded to include liberal arts studies and in 1872 was moved to

Minneapolis, Minnesota. The college became coeducational in 1922.

Augustana College at Sioux Falls, South Dakota, is the oldest college of the Evangelical Lutheran Church, dating back to 1860.

Concordia College at Moorhead, Minnesota, came into being in 1891 under the auspices of the Northwestern Lutheran College Association for the purpose of giving instruction to the sons and daughters of the pioneers. During the last few years Concordia has successfully conducted foreign language education for children and teenagers through summer camps which have attracted national and international attention. The camps have concentrated on the teaching of Norwegian, French, German, Spanish, Russian and Chinese languages. Following the purchase of a large tract of land near Bemidji, Minnesota, all of the language camps are now located together. Eventually each will have its own "village" within the camp area.

Thirty-four universities and nineteen colleges in the United States now have Scandinavian departments where Norwegian language, literature and history have been taught since 1858. In 1911 the Society for the Advancement of Scandinavian Studies was formed in Chicago, Illinois.

Instruction in Norwegian is also provided through a substantial number of classes and camps all over the country. These are primarily sponsored by the largest organization of Americans and Canadians of Norwegian birth, affiliation or descent, Sons of Norway. Headquartered in Minneapolis, Minnesota, Sons of Norway has some two hundred sixty local lodges in North America. Sons of Norway grants scholarships for participation in these camps as well as in the International Summer School of the University of Oslo.

The Press—In and Outside Norway

THE PRESS—IN AND OUTSIDE NORWAY

THERE ARE nearly four million Norwegians with four million opinions, so the saying goes. Quite a few of these reactions and attitudes are reflected daily in the Letters To The Editor columns of the newspapers. Some frustrated letter-writers, whose "Worried Father," "Irritated Taxpayer," "Anti-something-or-another" opinions did not get into print, have been known to start their own papers just to get their messages across. Over the years, since 1765 when the first Norwegian newspaper appeared, this trend has resulted in ranking the Norwegians as one of the most newspaper-minded people in the world, with an average of 2.1 papers per capita. In addition, Norwegians are avid subscribers to periodicals, notably illustrated weeklies catering to the whole family: *Norsk Ukeblad, Allers, Illustrert, Hjemmet;* to the ladies: *Alle Kvinners Blad, Det Nye, Kvinner og Klär, Romantikk;* to men: *Vi Menn, Alle Menn, Western, Detektivmagasinet;* and to the children of all ages, Donald Duck. Almost every profession, trade or organization of any size has its own periodical.

Historically, the development of the newspapers is closely tied in with the 1814 events at the village of Eidsvoll, where the Assembly adopted the new Constitution on May 17. From a prolonged, rather insignificant period due to dependence on Denmark, the Norwegian press slowly but steadily assumed a key position in the national

community. Culturally, the country underwent a romantic
renaissance spearheaded by poets like Henrik Wergeland
and Johan Sebastian Welhaven; writers like Henrik Ibsen
and Bjørnstjerne Bjørnson; composers such as Edvard
Grieg and Richard Nordraak; and painters like Adolph
Tiedemand, Hans Gude, and Christian Krohg. This development is well stated by Halvdan Koht and Sigmund
Skard in their book, *The Voice of Norway*.

". . . What happened in Norway in 1814 was virtually
a revolution. A small nation arose against the dictate of
the Great Powers and snatched its national independence.
By the same effort it passed from firmly-vested absolut-
ism to full-fledged democracy. The feat was the more remarkable since it happened at a moment when reaction
seized power in all the rest of Europe.

"It is still more remarkable that during the period of
reaction that followed the same small nation managed not
only to preserve the results of its courageous revolt, but
even to strengthen and enlarge its democracy. The vigor
and vitality developed in Norway immediately after the
strain of 1814 attests to a stock of energy accumulated
in the people through centuries. Both in individuals and
in society as a whole, creative forces were released that
worked as well for national solidarity as for spiritual liberty. Politics and literature joined vigorously in further-
ing this progress. . . ."

Organized political parties, forces previously unknown,
began to emerge. The first attempts were made among
the farmers who were striving to capture as many seats as
possible in the Storting. The labor movement, inspired by
the French February Revolution in 1848, was headed by
the school teacher Marcus Thrane who advocated reforms
such as universal suffrage, old age pensions and the cot-
ter system. Johan Sverdrup introduced a new orientation

in a leftist, liberal direction. In the same year, 1884, the conservative elements were also organized in a party on a national basis. These currents and cross-currents in the stormy political Norwegian atmosphere were bound to create an ever-stronger press easily defined by party affiliations. While there were only seventy papers in the late 1860's, the number had increased to more than one hundred thirty fifteen years later, in addition to about one hundred periodicals. Only the dailies in major cities could, however, afford to employ journalists on a full-time scale, but as circulations grew, the quality of publishing improved. The staffs became more skilled and the role and influence of the press increased substantially. Most dailies are still very much party-minded. Unlike editorials found in most American papers, which address themselves to the readership, those in the Norwegian press attack more bluntly and aggressively those appearing in the opposition camp. The discussions along these lines have been known to become rather ludicrous. In one small town, the two local editors had been trading insults editorially for quite some time. The original issue had been almost forgotten in the heat of the battle. As colleagues they always met over a cup of coffee in the afternoon, amiably discussing matters of joint professional interest. However, this did not prevent them from renewing their running battle in the next edition.

One morning Editor A discovered that an expected supply of newsprint had not yet arrived. He immediately called Editor B and asked if he would help him out. "Certainly," B replied to his colleague in distress and promptly dispatched the needed quantity. He was, however, not too amused next morning when A really gave him a broadside of every known invective in the Norwegian language, implemented with a few choice ones from Swedish and Dannish to bring his point across. Editor B's somewhat bitter retort was presented along these lines: ". . . it is bad enough to be insulted by an inferior person like Editor A, but to be insulted on one's own paper, that really does it! We are happy to inform our readers that Mr. A yesterday called us and begged for help to be able to issue his so-called newspaper. He told us that he had ordered and paid for a supply of newsprint, but we sincerely doubt that he is in a financial position to continue his miserable career. As a matter of fact, the last time we found something good in his paper was a couple of days ago, when two pounds of cod were wrapped in it. . . ."

We hasten to add that such an argumentation is not too common in the Norwegian press. On the contrary, the press generally presents an objective and cultured front of factual information, a well-balanced reporting on current events, and as a whole, mirrors opinions in a constructive, enlightening way. There are no Sunday papers in Norway and during long holidays, such as Christmas and Easter, the only news-disseminating media are radio and television. Attempts have been made to allow Sunday editions but negotiations have been unsuccessful, mainly due to the resistance of the carriers.

Out of more than one thousand six hundred publications about one hundred sixty are newspapers. The largest one is Oslo's conservative *Aftenposten,* which today has a circulation of approximately 350,000. It is followed by the liberal *Dagbladet,* also published in Oslo; the liberal *Bergens Tidende,* published in Bergen; the conservative *Adresse-Avisen* in Trondheim; the chief labor paper *Arbeiderbladet,* Oslo, and the *Verdens Gang,* also published in Oslo.

Norwegian journalists are organized into the *Norsk Presseforbund,* headquartered in Pressens Hus in Oslo.

The central agency for news and photo distribution is *Norsk Telegrambyraa,* which began its service in 1867 and since 1918 has been wholly owned by the newspapers. The agency is politically completely independent. It is run by newspapermen and cooperates closely with foreign news services, employing its own correspondents in key cities abroad as well as throughout Norway.

The foreign language press in America today consists of about six hundred publications, representing thirty-five language groups. They cover a market of 35 million people, particularly in the northwestern area. About seventy of these publications are dailies. In this connection it should be remembered that at least 15 million Americans continue to use a language other than English in their homes. The circulation and size of these publications graphically show that they generally followed the curve of the immigration waves during the last two centuries. The very first non-English publication was the German bimonthly, *Die Philadelphische Zeitung.* It was issued on May 6, 1732, by none other than Benjamin Franklin. It lasted only through two issues. The first newspaper in French, *Le Courrier de Boston,* was published in Boston, Massachusetts in 1789, and the first in Spanish, west of the Mississippi, *El Crepusculo* was printed in Taos, New Mexico in 1835. Twenty years after the opening of the large-scale Norwegian migration to America, the first newspaper appeared. It was named *Nordlyset* (Northern Lights) and was published for the first time in 1847 in Wisconsin. The Declaration of Independence and the Norwegian Constitution of 1814 were both featured in the initial issue. At about the same time another paper, *Skandinavia,* was issued in New York. Altogether there have been seven hundred papers and periodicals in the Norwegian language in America. More than one hundred fifty were

started in Minneapolis, Minnesota. Most of them lasted
five years or less and some died within one year. Only
ten survived for thirty years. Today there are five papers
using the Norwegian language: *Decorah-Posten,* Decorah,
Iowa; *Nordisk Tidende,* Brooklyn, New York; *Minnesota-
Posten,* Minneapolis, Minnesota; *Vinland,* Chicago, Illinois and *Western Viking,* Seattle, Washington. In Canada, the *Norrona* is published in Vancouver. Each one may
point with pride to a colorful history and background.
Each one is still doing an important service to the promotion and preservation of the Norwegian-American cultural
heritage and to the interests of maintaining the channels
between Norway and Norwegian America and Canada.
Other publications in the English language, such as the
Sons of Norway *Viking,* the *American Scandinavian Re-
view* and the *Norwegian American Commerce* are joining
forces with these Norwegian language newspapers to support this common cultural cause. The Norwegian language
press has been an important link between the Old Country
and America. The press has always provided timely information about America, interpreted the new and often
puzzling way of life, and voiced and shaped opinions. The
newspaper of the immigrant became a guide to help him
sink his roots ever deeper in the American community.
The Norwegian language press has performed at least
three essential functions. Using his native language, it
has schooled the newcomer in democratic principles and
institutions and thus helped him to prepare for full
participation in American life. It has been instrumental in
preserving some of the former patterns and finally it has
helped to spark American progress. The press emerged
out of the interplay among the various Norwegian-American groups of interests as the coordinating element. The
pressure of the total American process toward integration

is constantly felt. In this perspective the Norwegian-American press has a continuing importance and mission.

Traditions Never Die

TRADITIONS NEVER DIE

MAY 17 . . . THE DAY OF DAYS

THE RECIPE for an old-fashioned, genuine Norwegian *Syttende Mai* (Seventeenth of May) would be something like a dash of Fourth of July, a splash of a St. Patrick's Day Parade, songs by St. Olaf College Choir, music by Luther College Band, flags, flags and more flags, red-white-blue ribbons up to knee-length, Sunday clothes — and then children, heaps of children, all the children you are able to round up, all ages, all types — the more the merrier. Mix all this with salvos of gunpowder which explode and deafen your ears in order to assure yourself that it is by no means an ordinary day at all, but *Syttende Mai* — the day of days.

It was termed "The Blessed of all Days" by the great nationalist Henrik Wergeland, who is credited with starting the annual celebrations way back in the last century to commemorate the anniversary date of the Constitution of Norway adopted at Eidsvoll in 1814.

Amid shouts of hurrah, up go the flags. Caught by the spring wind they blossom forth all over the land and everywhere in the world where Norwegians live and work, even on board Norwegian ships on the high seas. Norway herself is at her very prettiest this time of the year. The greenness of spring blends well with the national colors and with the black-tasseled red caps of the graduating gym-

nasium students, who from now until graduation day are
entitled to behave in a way unbecoming to the rest of the
population.

Then comes the local band bursting with energy and
fortified by a solid morning meal. This is the moment for
which the band members have been waiting and training
the whole year, the end product of so many nights of rig-
orous rehearsals that kept them away from their wives,
children, televisions and card tables. This is their true hour
of glory. They have taken the loyalty oath that nobody but
nobody shall escape the presentation of any noted composer of marches on this day.

Some bands are financially supported by municipal
funds and therefore consist of more or less hand-picked
musical talents; others are made up of workers in a factory, clerks and secretaries in a firm, or employees in a
department store. They work together, so why not play
together? And this they do—uptown, downtown, cross-
town — everywhere, along streets and avenues, in city
squares, in front of and inside hospitals, old age homes
and children's homes. You name it, and they will be there
rendering their version. On one occasion the band from
the Steelworkers Union, after exploiting all marching
routes available in their own town, decided to invade the
neighboring city for some more musicmaking. There, however, the musicians ran into the band from the local Ironworkers Union, whose players did not exactly appreciate
the idea of seeing strangers encroach on their territory!
The ensuing clash between steelworkers and ironworkers
employing their instruments, primarily the tubas and trom-
bones, in a manner not exactly envisioned by composers,
still rings in the annals of the more memorable *Syttende
Mai* celebrations in Norway!

Not far from the bands is a group of more serious look-

ing gentlemen with top hats and women with tricolored
ribbons amidst all their finery. They constitute the official
committee assigned by the City Council to place a wreath
on the grave or monument of the local delegate to the
Eidsvoll Assembly of 1814, where it all began. For the
speaker, usually the city's representative at the *Storting* or
Parliament, the main point to bring across is that the
local Eidsvoll man was really someone special, as compared with Eidsvoll men from other places. As a matter
of fact, he informs his beaming audience, it would be
highly doubtful that anything of real national importance,
such as independence from Denmark, would have come
about at all had it not been for the right speech at the
right time made by the local delegate during the critical
hours at Eidsvoll. The speaker couldn't be more right,
the audience agrees. Now comes another series of hurrahs
and nods of the head in the direction of the great-great-
great grandson of the Eidsvoll delegate, the annual guest
of honor at this ceremony. They might not have voted
for him at the last municipal elections or otherwise en-
couraged his own political ambitions, but today, on this
day of days, he is entitled to every possible form of recognition. Forgetting his stunning political defeat, he will
now step forward, "speaking on behalf of my family . . ."
The City Song is rendered with fervor, all eighteen verses,
each extolling some specific local historical achievement,
such as thrashing the soccer team of the neighboring town
11-1, or commemorating the day when the fire department unveiled its first American-built fire engine. Of
course, they happily forget the minor incident when the
fire department set fire to a house which was condemned
anyway in order to demonstrate the new mechanical mar-
vel, and five or six other houses also went up in flames.
Eighteen verses are sung, as opposed to the City Song of

the town across the river which consists of only one verse, simply because there wasn't more to write about. With this satisfying thought in mind, everybody may now happily concentrate on the main event of the day: The Children's Parade.

Ah, what a lovely sight! All these myriads of children —flags and standards, bands and schools behind schools in alphabetical order, boy scouts and girl scouts, songs and cheers, a flowing multi-colored stream in rapid succession, a stampede of children whom the City Tax Collector reviews jubilantly, with an eye towards future tax revenues. Winding their way through the narrow streets and avenues, the children finally assemble in the City Square, where they confront the speaker of the day, another top hatted gentleman. He somewhat nervously fingers his numbered notes while waiting for the last strains of *Ja, vi elsker dette landet* to be carried away on the mild May breeze, gently reminding one and all that finally another glorious spring is embracing Norway. The speaker never forgets to inject this welcomed weather report before tackling the main subject: "Children! Fellow citizens! Compatriots!" . . . He asks everybody to look back in the past. Everybody does and happily agrees that it is quite a past; it has to be, filled as it is with Norwegians. A three-by-three hurrah for the past. Then he directs the attention to the future. The nation has quite a future in store. A three-by-three hurrah for the future. This leaves only the present and that is important too, the orator suggests, profoundly declaring that it is the present which links the past to the future. Another three-by-three, then more singing, more dancing, more games, free movies, sports contests, parties everywhere, fireworks — and another memorable *Syttende Mai* draws to a close.

As enthusiastically, almost feverishly as *Syttende Mai*

is celebrated in Norway, so is it equally set aside as a "no work-all fun" day all over the globe where native Norwegians or those of Norse descent live and work. It is celebrated on hundreds of Norwegian vessels on the high seas or in distant ports, in seamen's churches, in embassies and consulates, at private parties or with great parades attracting tens of thousands where the Norwegian "colonies" are of substantial size. This exuberant display of gaiety is perhaps more in evidence throughout the United States and Canada mainly because there are more Norse descendants in North America than in Norway and because the ties between the "Norway outside Norway" and the "Old Country" are in many ways stronger than similar relations between other ethnic groups and their respective ancestral countries. As it has once been stated, "The Norwegian immigrant is as fond of the Old Country as of his mother, and of the New Country as of his wife, and never is this unique loyalty so clearly expressed as it is on the 17th of May."

As the mainstream of Norwegian immigration more or less followed a basic axis stretching from New York and New Jersey, through Wisconsin, Illinois, the Upper Midwest states, to the Northwest Pacific states and California, so have May 17 celebrations always had the largest dimensions in these areas. Since the turn of the century huge crowds have participated in parades and programs in Brooklyn, New York and Chicago. Sons of Norway lodges together with other organizations and societies of Norse origin have spearheaded and arranged annual festivities in every community where Norwegian-Americans and Norwegian-Canadians are solidly represented. Proclamations are issued by the governors and mayors of such states and cities, and flowers are placed wherever there is a monument or a grave of a particularly noted Norwegian or Norwegian-American, for instance: Leif Erikson in several cities and violinist Ole Bull in Minneapolis.

In Norway *Syttende Mai* also marks an awakening of new life after the long cold winter months. In several cities, particularly in northern Norway, the return of the sun is hailed with sun pageants in which everybody merrily joins. Perhaps the most famous one is celebrated at the city of Rjukan, situated in a narrow valley, hemmed in by mountains six thousand feet high. Rjukan never sees the sun from late fall to the middle of March. The highlight of the sun pageant is the arrival of the "Prince of the Sun," accompanied by young maidens. He ascends his throne in the center of the Market Square where the mayor of Rjukan presents him with the mayoral Chain-of-Office. The Prince then issues the Order of the Day: "Let there be Merriment until Dawn." Old and young join in the open-air carnival, dressed in fancy costumes. There is dancing, entertainment and fireworks with the Prince himself entertaining his visitors and court.

MIDSUMMER

The Midsummer Night and Day—the 23rd and 24th of June—are called *Jonsok* or also *Sankt Hans,* both named after John the Baptist. However, the roots of this special celebration surrounding the shortest night and the longest day of the year reach all the way back to pagan times, when everybody paid tribute to the powers of the sun god with bonfires signifying the defeat of darkness. In addition, it was as good an excuse as any for a bit of "whooping-up," knowing as they did that soon the long, dark fall and winter months would engulf them. And on this night out of the deep forests, down from the mountains, up from the rivers and fjords would come the magic creatures—the trolls, the *hulders,* the *nisser,* the *fosse-*

grimer and the *nøkker*—invisible partners in all this merrymaking. The witches in particular had a very busy itinerary. Their destination that night was *Bloksberg,* where they were guests of *Gamle-Erik* (the Devil himself), and no Norwegian *heks* (witch) worthy of her profession and with any self-respect at all would miss being a delegate to that annual event. Using *sopelimer* (long-handled brooms) as transportation, the ride went swiftly, and since they all had to be back in Norway before sunrise, one must assume that the *Bloksberg* summit meeting was rather brief, concentrating perhaps on how to make life still more miserable for the Norwegians. The Norwegians in turn had a more serious matter to attend to through the Midsummer Night; they had to meet once more their departed relatives and friends who had left their graves to go into the church at the stroke of midnight. The procedure was to take a position close to the church, with a piece of sod on the head (representing the shared burden of the dead under the peat) and a hymn book closely pressed to the body. While the processions went by, not one word could be uttered, not one move made. At sunrise they were permitted to single out the departed ones from their own family and exchange a few pleasantries and news items before bidding good-bye. They were not allowed however to reveal anything of the conversation to anybody.

ST. OLAV'S DAY

Olsok, on July 29, is a day when the saintly Viking king Olav is honored with bonfires and historical plays at Stiklestad near the old capital city of Trondheim, where he fell in battle in the year 1030. Afterwards when it was discovered that his hair and nails were still growing, he was sainted.

UNITED NATION'S DAY

Norway, being a charter member of the United Nations and having the honor of her own statesman Trygve Lie being first Secretary General of the world organization, takes particular pride in marking October 24 as United Nation's Day.

. . . A CHRISTMAS IS A CHRISTMAS IS JUL

Nowhere in the world is Christmas more thoroughly celebrated and enjoyed than in Norway, where it is a remarkable blend of religious ritual and pagan rites. This fact is expressed in a popular ditty saying: *Nå er det jul igjen, nå er det jul igjen, og jula varer ratt til påske!* (Here it's Christmas again, here it's Christmas again, and Christmas lasts all the way to Easter!) This might not be quite the case; but even though most Norwegians conclude with the "Day of the Three Wise Men," thirteen days after Christmas Eve, there are some who refuse to call it quits before the twentieth day after the Season began. The first holiday indication is the annual reminder from the postal authorities that it is time to send packages, letters and cards to the tens of thousands of relatives manning the ships of Norway on the seven seas, not to mention a Norwegian possession such as Jan Mayen, the island between Iceland and Spitzbergen, where the mailman calls only once a year. Then, in late November, plain main streets turn into *julegater* (yule streets), with all the proper embellishment and extra lighting, to remind everybody that Christmas is only a few weeks away. By then many a Norwegian has written a book for sale, and the book stores are stocked to capacity with volumes which are promptly sold. The Norwegians like to preserve their reputation as belonging to one of the world's most avid book-reading nations. Norway is, in fact, the country which annually has the greatest number of published book titles per capita. The total number of books printed every year is about 16 million. Today the sales are getting more evenly spread over the year, yet the pre-Christmas turn-over is still in the lead.

Christmas trees are plentiful in this country that is almost one quarter covered with forests, mostly spruce and pine. They are out for display and sale in market places and any vacant lot in sight. The biggest ones go to the University Square in Oslo, outside most public buildings everywhere, to churches, schools and hospitals. The Norwegians do not, however, stop at this point. For many years they have been sending giant trees as gifts to London, England, Reykjavik, Iceland, the Hague, Neth-erlands, and a number of other European cities as tokens of friendship and a willingness to share the Nor-wegian *jul* with everybody everywhere. Even the ships of Norwegian registry feature Christmas trees in their mast tops, wherever they may be during the holy season.

On the farm, the only one not looking forward to *jul* with any noticeable anticipation is the *julegrisen,* the pig, who by now has grown rather suspicious of all this fuss and unfailing attention paid him during the last few months. Only the best, it seems, has been good enough to feed him. The squealing excluded, all other parts of the pig are usable for the traditional holiday dishes, including the feet which are pickled in salt brine. As a final salute to such a noble animal providing so much culinary pleas-ure, the farmer and his helpers take a skoal for each of the bones in the pig's feet, said to number two dozen or so.

Along the kitchen front the activities are in full swing. No self-respecting Norwegian housewife would dream of being caught with her rolling pin down or less than seven different kinds of cookies in her jars. Some are still hoping to bake fourteen varieties, which, according to the old customs, means one kind for every day of the whole Christmas season. Among the cookies, one called *fattigmann* (poor man's cookie) requires ingredients such as high grade eggs, butter, sugar, vanilla, finest flour, heavy cream and cardamon (which might imply that the name of this cookie indicates the financial position of the baker after filling such a recipe!)

Rice porridge is a more or less standard feature of the national, traditional Christmas menu. Quite a few families serve it early in the day of Christmas Eve with a mixed-in almond nut. The lucky finder is awarded a special gift, in most cases a marzipan pig with a red ribbon. For centuries in rural Norway this porridge has had a very special purpose. Every farm has its own little tenant, an elf called *nissen*, who resides in the barn and on a year-round basis keeps an eye on everything and everybody. His annual reward is a bowl of rice porridge on Christmas Eve. If the bowl is found empty in the morning, all is indeed well, and the *nissen* has renewed his lease. If the porridge hasn't been touched, there is trouble ahead. The farmer could either take a chance and go on as before or emigrate to America. The good elf had apparently decided to move on to another farm.

The cattle, horses and other animals on the farm are taken extra good care of shortly before Christmas in order to avoid an unfavorable meeting at midnight Christmas Eve, when the animals are supposed to be able to speak and discuss the over-all impression of the farmer and his family. Even the birds are remembered. The largest and best sheaves of grain from the harvest are placed on poles out in the yard or on the roofs of the buildings. If the birds come in great numbers to enjoy this treat, the year ahead will be a good one.

At four o'clock in the afternoon on Christmas Eve the church bells start chiming all over Norway, jubilantly heralding that Christmas is here. Stores and offices close. Last-minute striped ties for father and uncles are purchased to complete the collection of gifts amassed under the gaily decorated Christmas trees in the living rooms. Most trees also have small Norwegian flags, and in homes where there are relatives living in America, similar small American flags will also be found on the trees. Norwegian children find it unthinkable to wait until Christmas morning for their gifts and have a rather skeptic attitude when it comes to the ability of *julenissen* — the Norwegian cousin of Santa Claus — to find his way down the chimney. They expect that all gifts have already been delivered by him and placed under the tree while they impatiently have been waiting outside for the tree to be trimmed and lighted. Or they have been on a *julebukk*-round, visiting house after house in the neighborhood, extending Christmas wishes and in return being treated with fresh-smelling cookies.

Before any gift is handed out, the family enjoys a solid Christmas dinner, and quite a meal it is. Some families go easy on the Christmas Eve supper in anticipation of the Christmas Day grand dinner. Then follows the traditional walk around the tree with singing of all the most beloved Christmas carols, such as:

> *Da tender moder alle lys,*
> *og ingen krok er mørk,*
> *hun sier stjernen lyste så*
> *i hele verdens ørk.*

> *Hun sier at den lyser enn*
> *og slukkes aldri ut,*
> *og hvis den skinner på min vei,*
> *da kommer jeg til Gud.*

Jeg holder av vår julekveld
og av den Herre Krist
og at han elsker meg igjen
det vet jeg ganske visst.

Then mother lights the Christmas tree
And fills the room with light.
She says that so the Star shone forth
And made the dark world bright;

She says the star is shining still,
And never will grow dim;
And if it shines upon my way,
It leads me up to Him.

And so I love each Christmas Eve,
And I love Jesus too;
And that He loves me in return,
I know so well is true.

Christmas Day morning is for church-going and in the evening relatives get together. Second Day Christmas, also a holiday, means another round of festivities—gatherings of relatives and friends at home or in restaurants or theatres.

The children particularly look forward to the most popular Christmas play, *Reisen til Julestjernen* (The Search for the Christmas Star), annually staged by the Norwegian National Theatre in Oslo and several other theatres throughout the country. It tells of a king and a queen who had only one beautiful little princess named Sonja Gulltopp. One day she was kidnapped by thieves. Her mother, the Queen, died of sorrow and when Christmas came, the King felt so lonely and grieved that he could not stand the sight of the Christmas Star shining above the palace. He banished the Star and it disappeared from the sky. Several years passed and the Princess had still not been found. One day some wise star-gazers came to the King. They had read in the stars that if only the Christmas Star shone again, the little Princess would also reappear. The King now offered a great reward for the one who could locate the Christmas Star and make it shine again. Once again thieves broke into the castle and among them was a young girl dressed in rags. They were caught but the King felt sorry for the girl and let her go. She was so thankful that she promised to find the Christmas Star. She set out on the search and had many adventures and difficulties but made friends with all the animals and birds in the forests who helped her when she was in trouble. One day she heard beautiful music and bells ringing in the forest. It was Christmas Eve; she knelt in the snow and prayed and unfastened a golden heart from around her neck. It had once been given to her by her mother and she now offered to give it to the Christmas Star if it would only shine again.

The miracle happened! While angels were singing, the bright Christmas Star slowly descended into the hands of the young girl. She carried it carefully to the Palace, again helped by animals. She even had a ride with the North Wind, visiting the home of Father Christmas, just as he was busy with wrapping all the Christmas presents for all the children in the world. Finally the girl could give the Star to the King and he then recognized the girl as his long-lost daughter.

The Christmas Star ascended again into the heavens, shining brighter than ever before.

COMPLICATED COURTSHIPS AND PROLONGED WEDDINGS

Anyone visiting Norway in anticipation of seeing a genuine, traditional three-to-four-day rural wedding will have to settle for more or less staged versions at folk festivals, such as the *Fana Folklore* at Bergen. All the pomp and glory of century-old traditions are here retained, with the beautifully embellished bridal crown, the national costumes, the fiddle players, the folk dances, the rosepainted ale bowls passed from guest to guest, and all the other merriment planned to put the bridal couple on the launching pad for presumably permanent connubial bliss. Today the everyday Norwegian courtship and wedding proceedings are like those found in most other countries.

The marriage is performed in church or City Hall, streamlined and simple, and above all, kept as private as possible for the two principals, their families and close friends. Lavish or low-budgeted, a Norwegian wedding today, be it urban or rural, is by and large a private occasion.

Not so seven hundred to eight hundred years ago. Then everybody got into the act, even the authorities. The boy-meets-girl concept was not quite accepted by society, even if they sometimes managed to get together on their own. Formally the father of the girl played the most important part as he decided whom his daughter should marry. If he passed away without having hand-picked a prospective son-in-law, the right to decide went to her brothers. This again frequently led to the rather awkward situation in which brother No. 1 promised his sister to one candidate, brother No. 2 or 3 at the same time having committed her to other prospects. Fortunately there was a solution, perfect in all its simplicity. They had a raffle among the lined-up swains, with the winner securing the bride, and the losers receiving a handsome cash compensation for breach of contract.

The bride-to-be never left her homestead empty-handed, but was endowed with the so-called *heimanfylgje,* the dowry of those times. It was strictly a personal gift. If she died, the money went back to her parents. Her husband, who had to match the *heimanfylgje* with a similar amount (only 50 percent if the bride was a widow), was in this case entitled to have his contribution refunded.

When all these financial details had been settled, the *festermålet* took place, with hand-shaking, back-slapping and eating and drinking of considerable quantities of home-made beer. The wedding took place in the bride-groom's house. Shortly before the ceremony the bride-groom, escorted by friends, arrived at his fiancee's house to pick her up. The presence of the escort was mainly intended to avoid any last-minute change of plans or sudden impulse, such as second thoughts on the part of the bride's father about the general qualities of the young man, or, for that matter, the whole prospective in-law clan. In that case, a peaceful solution might be found through another round of negotiations involving financial transactions in reverse, or an all-out feud, which might reverberate for at least two centuries. Fortunately such incidents were rather infrequent.

The timing was often as important as the wedding itself. No marriage could take place six weeks prior to or during Christmas. Neither could it take place within six weeks of Easter. For many reasons midsummer was practical as well as romantic and the most popular time for nuptials. Least favored was the fall after the frost had set in. Then the girl was called a "frosty bride," a label no young lady liked to have pinned on herself. Midsummer was most convenient for everybody; the sun was at its highest; nature was at her prettiest; the hay-making chores were still ahead; in short, everything was perfect for such an enjoyable social event as a wedding. And enjoy it they did for almost seven days and nights of continuing festivities, all centered around the young couple, the *kjøgemeister* (Norwegian version of a wedding master of ceremonies) and, last but not least, the fiddler. It was the fiddler who got things moving by extracting the first harsh sounds from his Hardanger fiddle, Norway's firm answer to Scotland's bagpipes. The unique and not altogether pleasant sound of his fiddle indicates why the Vikings might have settled in places like Ireland, Normandy, Iceland, Greenland and Vinland, and maybe also why the emigrants of more recent centuries left Norway in such large numbers as they did.

Meanwhile, back on the wedding farm, nobody seemed to mind. On the contrary, the fiddler, or any musician for that matter, was the most popular participant. Without him no *springar, halling,* or other folk dance could be properly executed by the people of those days. He also led the solemn procession to the church, probably to alert the minister that the young couple was ready for the ceremony.

For many years this took place outside the church. The minister had to assure himself first that the bride and groom were not too closely related in a forbidden way (such as being godfather and godmother to the same child). He also had to be completely convinced that this marriage was voluntarily entered into by both of them. Only one ring was used, handed by the groom to the pastor who kissed it and placed it on the bride's finger. Then the church doors were opened and the young couple escorted in by candle light. The regular service followed, but the text was carefully chosen to fit the wedding. Following the service the pastor joined the bridal procession back to the groom's home where the "blessing of the bed" took place in a very solemn manner, with the newlyweds kneeling in prayer while a hymn was sung.

On the second day the bride appeared in her *skaut,* the kerchief symbolizing that she now was indeed a married woman. She walked around with a big wooden bowl, collecting money as wedding gifts or pledges. Some brought food along for the wedding party, which often comprised several hundred guests. Housing during the wedding period also offered a serious problem. Every available attic, basement, barn and stable was occupied by guests badly in need of a little rest.

ETIQUETTE MEANS ". . . SSSSSST"

Customs and traditions in any land are not restricted to the events of importance either in the community or the family life. Customs develop to govern most of the human relations among the people. And in the development of such customs Norwegians have come to be known as the mightiest hand-shakers of the world. Thus a foreigner visiting in Norway will become accustomed to the sight of two or more hand-shaking Norwegians in any street in any town. If the visitor chooses to partake of this national pastime, he should not forget to include the ladies. If they should be neglected in a round of hand-shaking, they might suspect that they are carriers of some rare disease; they probably would not be aware of the fact that in the United States one rarely grabs a lady's hand, except perhaps when proposing.

What primarily will intrigue the visitor observing these commonplace street-scenes is the constant hissing sound accompanying this hand-to-hand movement. Don't assume that the handshakers are mad at each other. On the contrary, they are simply thanking each other *for sist,* which again means "last time" they met. Perhaps the occasion was a dinner party or some other major social event, which calls forth this expression of utter delight about the pleasure of being together again. *Sist,* thus, in the race for being the first one to say it, comes out like . . . *sssst!* In the

same way expressions such as *morn!* and *morn'a!* are
shortened versions of *god morgen* (good morning) and
ha en god morgen, da (have a good morning). Here
again the stranger might be somewhat puzzled by the fact
that regardless of the time of day or night, be it nine in
the morning, four in the afternoon, ten in the evening, or
any hour around the clock, he will constantly hear these
morn's *and morna*'s. Right now, however, he will at this
given moment be fully occupied by the hissing . . . *sssssts*
accompanied by broad smiles which indicate that it truly
must have been quite a party.

A formal dinner party is now most commonly preceded
by an invitation by phone. If invitation cards have been
sent out and a phone number listed, one may safely reply
by phone or accept with a written thank-you note. Invita-
tions to weddings, confirmation or anniversary dinners are
always by cards.

When dinner is announced, the host leads the parade
to the dining room, while the hostess is the last one to
enter. She has the guest of honor at her left side, while
the host escorts the wife of the guest of honor on his right
side. To his left is the oldest of the ladies present.

When everybody has been served wine and tasted the
soup or the first course, he welcomes the guests to the table.
The principle speech for the special guest is given after
a second helping of the main course has been served. The
host requests his guests to join him in a skoal for the main
guest, who remains seated while everybody else stands up.
When all has been said and done at the table, the honor of
saying *takk for maten* (thanks for the meal) is given to
the guest of honor, addressing himself to the hostess. In
the meantime everybody has toasted everybody by lifting
the glass and slightly nodding to the person singled out.
One must not, however, try to "catch the eye" of the

hostess for a toast. It would be a catastrophe if she would be obliged to respond to twenty or thirty skoals! When leaving the table, the guests line up for another round of handshaking with the host and hostess before moving on to the living room for coffee, which is served only rarely during the dinner.

*

As for state banquets or similar high-level social functions, the Norwegians adhere completely to the internationally accepted Vienna Code. This "ABC" in diplomatic conduct is in itself a fascinating document. It spells out every detail of behavior in the presence of the highest ranking persons. Inside as well as outside the corps diplomatique, it is "must" reading for any host and hostess about to entertain guests who have rows of orders, medals and other decorations on their upper left jacket side.

Just to enter a reception and/or dinner offers certain problems efficiently solved by the Vienna Code. If two enter, in the so-called lateral order (side by side), then the highest ranking official walks to the right of the lower ranking (2-1). If, however, three enter at the same time, the order will then be 3-1-2. Should the door be wide enough to accommodate a number of guests to enter at the same time, then we are faced with the following line-up:

4 persons: 3-1-2-4
5 persons: 5-3-1-2-4
6 persons: 5-3-1-2-4-6
7 persons: 7-5-3-1-2-4-6

If, however, the linear system is applied to the situation of room-entering, i.e. one person following behind another, then we face quite a different problem. The most exalted of the guest group will then enter first, with the second-ranking right behind him, and so on. This is fine provided none of the distinguished guests reconsiders and leaves for another social function. This might create havoc all around.

Before dinner some of the guests may feel inclined to sit down after a hard day of diplomatic chores. Here again the Code provides all the answers. If the sofa seats eight, the correct order with everybody in place then should be: 7-5-3-1-2-4-6-8. If No. 8 should then feel too embarrassed to be in such outstanding company, he might leave, which the others quite naturally will deem as an excellent idea, giving each one of them more space on the sofa, laterally as well as lineally.

Pomp and Circumstance

POMP AND CIRCUMSTANCE

NORWEGIANS, not unlike their other European neighbors, have always made much of flags and flag-waving. In fact a History of Norway could be read from a history of her flags.

The oldest is the Royal Standard, the flag of the head of state.

It is red, with a golden lion holding a silver axe and, as the coat-of-arms of the Kings of Norway, this emblem dates from about A.D. 1200. King Haakon IV used a lion on his shield, and so did his son King Magnus the Law-mender, whose successor King Erik Magnusson gave the emblem its final form in the year 1285. Since that date the lion has always been the Norwegian coat-of-arms.

From the end of the 14th century until the year 1814 Norway was united with Denmark; and the Danish flag, red with a white cross, was used also in Norway. Nevertheless, the old Norwegian Royal Standard appears to have been in use as a flag down to the 18th century, but mainly on some castles and naval vessels. By a decree of 1748, the Danish flag was formally declared to be the one legal merchant flag of the "twin kingdoms." It was also their naval flag, under which the great Norwegian eighteenth-century Admiral Peter Wessel Tordenskiold fought in the wars against Charles XII of Sweden. After the dissolution of the Union with Denmark in 1814, the

Danish flag was retained provisionally in Norway for a few years, but now the Norwegian lion was inserted in the upper left corner.

The present merchant flag of Norway was adopted in 1821. The form chosen was that of a cross, similar to the one found in the Danish and Swedish flags. The colors— red, white, and blue—were the "colors of freedom," the same as those of the United States and Great Britain, at that time almost the only countries of importance which were not ruled by absolute monarchs. The colors were also, significantly, those of the French tricolor, a revolutionary symbol, the showing of which was prohibited in France by the government of Louis XVIII. Quite apart from its political significance it was anything but beautiful, and its introduction aroused mixed feelings in Sweden as well as in Norway. It soon came to be commonly accepted, however, and remained in force for more than fifty years.

Toward the end of the nineteenth century, when Norwegians were growing increasingly impatient with their country's inferior position within the Union, a strong agitation was started to reintroduce the "pure" flag of Norway. A bill to this effect was duly passed by the Storting. Under the Constitution the King had a right, however, to veto twice any bills passed by the National Assembly. Only when, after two general elections, the "pure flag" bill went through the Storting for the third time in 1898, did it become law (without royal assent). For military purposes, the flag with the Union mark continued to be used until the dissolution of the Union between Sweden and Norway seven years later. The pure red, white and blue "State flag" was hoisted on all Norwegian fortresses and warships on June 9th, 1905. (The "State flag," for use on public buildings and naval vessels differs only in shape, with its swallow-tail and tongue.)

The old Norwegian Royal Standard, which had not been used by those who were kings of both Sweden and Norway, was hoisted on the Palace in the Norwegian capital after the election of the country's King Haakon VII, in November, 1905.

The history of the red, white and blue Norwegian flag is essentially a history of peace. Norwegians may have reason to be proud of what has been accomplished under this emblem, yet they will think primarily not of military exploits, but of economic expansion in fields such as shipping and whaling, or of the peaceful conquest of the globe through the deeds of Arctic explorers like Fridtjof Nansen and Roald Amundsen. Or again they may think of daring expeditions like the one that brought Thor Heyerdahl and his followers under this flag, in 1947, across the Pacific Ocean on a tiny raft, the Kon-Tiki.

Norway has had the good fortune to be at peace with other countries for 130 out of the 150 years that have passed since the adoption of her flag. It should not be forgotten, however, that for five years, during the Second World War, Norwegians fought under this flag to preserve the freedom of their country.

Alfred Bernhard Nobel was a Swede, the inventor of dynamite and the instigator and the provider for the Nobel prizes which bear his name.

He certainly surprised quite a few of his fellow Swedes and most Norwegians when he decided in 1895 that the Peace Prize should be distributed by Norway while the four other prizes, for physics, chemistry, medicine and literature, were placed in the hands of Swedish institutions. His action came at a time when relations between Sweden and Norway were extremely strained, almost to the breaking-point. A number of issues, particularly in the conduct

of foreign affairs, had shaken the foundations of the union
and at times brought the two countries to the verge of
war. Mr. Nobel might have considered his decision a contribution toward the avoidance of such a calamity between
two nations which had so much in common, historically
and culturally. He was an admirer of the works and actions of Norway's great writer and national figure of that
time, Bjørnstjerne Bjørnson. Perhaps this also influenced
his decision to leave the implementation of this part of
his will to the Storting, the Norwegian Parliament. The
clause states: "A committee of five persons to be elected
by the Norwegian Storting is to award annually one share
of the income of the fund to the person who shall have
most or best promoted the fraternity of nations and the
abolishment or reduction of standing armies, and the formation and extension of peace congresses."

Six years later the Nobel Committee adopted its official
designation — The Norwegian Storting's Nobel Committee.
On December 10th of that year, the anniversary of the
death of Nobel, the first Prize went to Jean Henri Dunant,
the founder of the Red Cross, and Frederic Passy, a co-
founder of the Inter-Parliamentary Union. Since then the
Prize has gone to more than sixty persons, organizations,
and institutions; it has been withheld several times.

The following Americans and Canadians have received
the Peace Prize: In 1906, President Theodore Roosevelt
for negotiating peace between the Russians and Japanese;
in 1912, Elihu Root, U.S. Secretary of State, for organizing the Central American Peace Conference and solving
the problem of Japanese immigration on the West Coast;
in 1919, President Woodrow Wilson for advocating the
League of Nations; in 1925 U.S. Vice-President Charles
G. Dawes for his German reparations payments plan; in
1929, Frank B. Kellogg, U.S. Secretary of State for nego-

tiating the Kellogg-Briand pact; in 1931, Jane Addams, president of the Women's International League for Peace, and Nicholas M. Butler, for his Carnegie Endowment for International Peace work; in 1945, Cordell Hull, U.S. Secretary of State, for peace efforts; in 1946, John R. Mott for his YMCA work, and Emily Balch for her work as President of the Women's International League for Peace and Freedom; in 1947, the American Friends Service Committee for humanitarian work. In 1950 the Prize went to Ralph Bunche, Under-Secretary of the United Nations, as mediator in Palestine in 1948-1949; in 1953, to George C. Marshall, U.S. Secretary of State, for the European Recovery Program (the Marshall Aid); in 1957 to Lester B. Pearson, Canadian Prime Minister, for his contribution to the organizing of a U.N. Force in Egypt; in 1962, Professor Linus Pauling for his promotion of peaceful use of nuclear energy; in 1964, to the Reverend Martin Luther King for his civil rights efforts; and in 1970 to Dr. Norman A. Borlaug (of Norwegian descent) for his agricultural achievements. Secretary of State Henry Kissinger received the Nobel award in 1973. Two Norwegians have also been honored with the Peace Prize: Fridtjof Nansen in 1922 for his relief work with Russian prisoners of war and starving people in the Russian famine area (the Nansen passport) and, in 1921, Christian L. Lange, secretary general of the Inter-Parliamentary Union. Over the years, other Norwegians have received the Nobel Prize in literature, science, and related fields.

Those qualified to recommend candidates for the Peace Prize are members and former members of the Nobel Committee and advisors named by the Norwegian Nobel Institute; members of parliaments and cabinets of any nation; members of the Inter-Parliamentary Union; members of the International Arbitration Court, the Hague,

Netherlands; members of the Council of the Permanent Peace Bureau, Geneva, Switzerland; members and associates of the Institute de Droit International; university professors of political science and law, of history and philosophy, and finally persons who have received the Nobel Peace Prize. Direct personal applications are not taken into consideration.

In addition to the Nobel Peace Prize, the Norwegian Government awards several of its own. The Military Cross was instituted in 1914; the St. Olav Medal (1939) is awarded for exceptional services in spreading knowledge about Norway abroad. King Haakon VII's Freedom Cross is awarded as a recognition of distinguished service to Norway during World War II. The same is true for the Military Medal (1941), King Haakon VII's Freedom Medal, and the Service Medal, which was given to all who saw service during the 1940 campaign in Norway.

The Constitution of Norway states: "The Kingdom of Norway is a free, independent, indivisible and inalienable realm. Its form of Government is a limited and hereditary monarchy. . . . The Executive Power is vested in the King. . . . The King shall always profess the Evangelical-Lutheran religion, and maintain and protect the same. . . . The King's person shall be sacred; he cannot be blamed nor accused. The responsibility rests with his Council. . . . The order of succession shall be lineal and agnatic, whereby only male, born in lawful wedlock, may succeed male; the nearer line shall pass before the more remote, and the elder in the line before the younger. Among those entitled to the succession shall be considered also an unborn child, who shall immediately take his proper place in the line of succession the moment he is born into the world after the death of his father. . . . If there is no Prince entitled to the succession, the King may propose his successor to the Storting (Parliament) which has the right to elect another candidate if the King's nominee is not acceptable. . . . As soon as the King, being of full age, assumes the authority of Government, he shall make to the Storting the following oath: 'I promise and swear that I will govern the Kingdom of Norway in accordance with its Constitution and Laws, so truly help me God, the Almighty and Omniscient!' "

The Constitution also states (No. 108): "No earldoms, baronies, majorats or fideicommissa may be created in the future."

When the Union with Sweden was dissolved on June 7, 1905, the keen bitterness felt by many Norwegians against the Swedish King had created a substantial sentiment for a new form of government in terms of a Republic. The great majority of the Storting was, however, in favor of a continued monarchy, and the Crown of Norway was offered to the young Danish Prince Carl. He accepted but demanded a plebiscite in order to be fully sure that the people really wanted him. The popular vote was held in November, 1905 when 259,563 voted in favor of a monarchy, and 69,264 against. Prince Carl then accepted the royal dignities offered him by a unanimous Storting, and adopted the name of Haakon VII. On November 25, 1905, he entered the Norwegian capital with his British-born Queen Maud and their two-year old son Alexander, now named Olav.

During his reign King Haakon VII was highly respected for his strength of character, dignified behavior and political clear-sightedness. Above all he was an *elected* sovereign by a democratic people who still were feeling their way into the 20th century after so many centuries of dependency. His own innate personal modesty and quiet humor contributed to the building of his people's affection.

There are many stories told which reflect King Haakon's fine traits. Once, during a stroll through the Palace park, he met a little girl with a camera. She asked if she might take a picture of her king but soon gave up. "You are too tall," she said, "I can't get you into my camera." "Why don't you take me in two sections?" His Majesty smilingly suggested.

King Haakon's wisdom, loyalty and allegiance to the Constitution evoked not only the admiration but also a deeply felt love for him during the Nazi invasion and occupation of Norway. In the truest sense of the word he then became the leader of his people, the symbol of freedom. He was the incarnation of Norway's nationhood and at his death in 1957 everyone mourned a personal loss.

Norway had also taken to her heart the two-year-old boy, Crown Prince Olav, when he was carried ashore on his father's arm that misty November day in 1905. The nation watched the boy mature into a strong young man, who, as the years went by, amply rewarded the love and respect bestowed upon him by his manly deeds, completely worthy of an heir to an ancient saga throne. He was brought up like any other typical Norwegian youngster, yet his parents and tutors always kept an eye on the fact that his education had to be adapted to his future royal responsibilities. When he came of age in 1924, he stated, ". . . I want especially to thank my parents because they understood the importance of letting me go to the same schools and acquire the same education as so many other Norwegian boys. I'm also grateful because they let me take in so many sports. This means that I came in close contact with so many people in this country, whose destiny and future are so close to my own. . . ."

This close contact was in evidence right from the beginning. He took part in ski jumping contests, winning several fine prizes. He defended the Norwegian colors at many international regattas, where only the very top sailors stood any chance, and took an active interest in many other athletic fields. The enthusiasm of the Norwegian people for their Crown Prince mounted steadily and the genuine popularity he enjoyed was by no means based on sheer politeness but admiration for his personal qualities. His most severe test as a leader came with the Nazi invasion in April, 1940, and he truly rose in a magnificent manner to the challenge. When the Royal Family and the Government had to leave occupied Norway, the Crown Prince offered to stay behind with the isolated people. It was finally decided that he should go along to England. Through his personal activities during World War II the capable Crown Prince rendered a valuable physical and moral service not only to the fighting free forces of Norway, but also to the Home Front inside his native country. Constantly on the move, inspecting, inspiring and guiding, he shared the hardships with his fellow-countrymen and he shared the final triumphs, climaxed by the day of another historic June 7, in 1945. Because the Prince returned in May, he was able to welcome his royal father, the King, back on liberated Norwegian soil. Never had any Prince of Norway been so close to the hearts of a people as he was then.

Victories had followed defeats; justice triumphed. The King was back in his Palace and the Crown Prince reunited with his wife, Crown Princess Märtha and their three children who had spent the war years as the guests of President Franklin D. Roosevelt in the United States. This happy reunion reflected the happiness of tens of thousands of other families throughout the whole country.

Therefore, when in 1957 he succeeded his late father, it was truly as a people's king. The nation had been deeply saddened when his wife, a Swedish Princess, died in 1954.

His daughters, Ragnhild and Astrid, both married commoners but have retained their titles as Princesses.

When his son, Crown Prince Harald, was born in 1937, nearly 600 years had passed since the last time a prince was born in Norway. Accordingly the birth was celebrated by the people of the country as an important historical event. Like his father, Prince Harald is an eminent yachtsman. And in 1968 he, like his sisters, married a commoner. She is now the Crown Princess Sonja and was formerly Sonja Haraldsen of Oslo. They have two children, a daughter, Märtha Louise, born in 1971, and a son, Haakon Magnus, born in 1973.

The Royal Palace in Oslo, overlooking the main street, Karl Johans Gate, was finished for use in 1848. Very extensive modernization and rebuilding work have been undertaken to make the building more representative, up-to-date, and livable. Crown Prince Harald and the Crown Princess reside in the village of Asker near Oslo at the Skaugum estate, a wedding gift from Ambassador Fritz Wedel Jarlsberg to the parents of the Crown Prince. The estate has a magnificent location with a beautiful view of the Oslofjord. The Royal Manor at Bygdøy, also close to Oslo, is the closest modern version of the *kongsgård* of the fairy tales, a peaceful and idyllic place near the Norwegian Folk Museum. This pleasant white building from the 1770s was the favorite residence of King Haakon VII and Queen Maud. Not far from this "King's Farm" is the *Oscarshall,* today more or less a curiosity, built in the neo-Gothic style. It is rather infrequently used by the King for summer receptions.

Outside Oslo there are a number of residences for the Royal Family, but they are state properties put at the disposal of the Royal Family rather than private property.

These include the *Stiftsgaarden* in the city of Trondheim, one of the largest wooden buildings in Europe, containing seventy rooms; the *Gamlehaugen* in Bergen, which once belonged to the Prime Minister Christian Michelsen, a key figure when the Union with Sweden was dissolved in 1905; *Ledaal* in Stavanger, once the home of the famed Norwegian writer, Alexander Kielland; and, in addition, several sports cabins in the mountains and at the sea, reflecting the keen yachting interest of all the members of the Royal Family. Hardly a residence but nevertheless a most comfortable and convenient accommodation for the King is the Royal Yacht "Norge," a gift from the Norwegian people to King Haakon VII. King Olav uses this elegant 1,612-ton yacht so often in national and foreign waters that she might perhaps be called another royal residence.

Although it is not the National Anthem of Norway, the Norwegian Royal Anthem is frequently sung by Norwegians everywhere to honor their king. The melody is the same as that for the English anthem, "God Save the King."

> *Gud sign vår Konge god,*
> *sign ham med kraft og mot,*
> *sign hjem og slott.*
> *Lys for ham ved din ånd,*
> *knytt med din sterke hånd*
> *hellige troskapsbånd*
> *om folk og drott.*
>
> *Høyt sverger Norges mann,*
> *hver i sitt kall, sin stand*
> *troskap sin drott.*
> *Trofast i liv og død,*
> *tapper i krig og nød,*
> *alltid vårt Norge lød*
> *Gud og sin drott.*

God save our gracious King,
Grant him in everything
Courage and power.
Guide him each waking hour,
On him thy blessings shower,
In closer union bring
People and King.

Norwegians everywhere
Steadfast allegiance swear
Unto their King.
Faithful in death and life,
Valorous in peace and strife,
Forever following
God and their King.

In recalling the history of the nation, the reader might be guided by this list of the Kings of Norway:

The Viking Kings of Norway 900-1380

Harald Fairhair (Harald I)	900- 940
Erik Bloodaxe (Erik I)	940- 945
Haakon the Good (Haakon I)	945- 960
Harald Graypelt (Harald II)	960- 970
Earl Haakon	970- 995
Olav Tryggvason (Olav I)	995-1000
Earls Erik and Svein	1000-1016
Olav Haraldson (St. Olav, Olav II)	1016-1030
Canute the Great (Prince Svein Alfivason regent)	1030-1035
Magnus the Good (Magnus I)	1035-1047
Harald Hardråde (Harald III)	1047-1066
Olav the Peaceful (Olav III)	1066-1093
Magnus Bareleg (Magnus III)	1093-1103
Eystein Magnusson (Eystein I)	1103-1125

Sigurd Magnusson the Crusader (Sigurd I)   1125-1130
Harald Gilchrist (Harald IV)   1130-1136
Magnus Sigurdson the Blind (Magnus III)   1136-1138
Inge Haraldson (Inge I)
Sigurd Haraldson (Sigurd II)   1138-1161
Eystein Haraldson (Eystein II)
Haakon Sigurdson (Haakon II)   1161-1162
Magnus Erlingson (Magnus IV)   1163-1184
Sverre Sigurdson   1184-1202
Haakon Sverreson (Haakon III)   1202-1204
Inge Baardson (Inge II)   1204-1217
Haakon Haakonson (Haakon IV)   1217-1263
Magnus Haakonson the Lawmender
  (Magnus V)   1263-1280
Erik Magnusson (Erik II)   1280-1299
Haakon Magnusson (Haakon V)   1299-1319
Magnus Erikson (Magnus VI)   1319-1355
  (Personal union with Sweden)
Haakon Magnusson (Haakon VI)   1355-1380

Kings of Denmark and Norway 1380-1814
Olav Haakonson (Olav IV)   1380-1387
Queen Margaret   1387-1412
Erik of Pomerania (Erik III)   1389-1442
Christopher of Bavaria   1442-1448
Christian I   1448-1481
Hans   1481-1513
Christian II   1513-1523
Frederik I   1523-1533
Christian III   1537-1559
Frederik II   1559-1588
Christian IV   1588-1648
Frederik III   1648-1670
Christian V   1670-1699

Frederik IV	1699-1730
Christian VI	1730-1746
Frederik V	1746-1766
Christian VII	1766-1808
Frederik VI	1808-1814

Christian Frederik, King of Norway, May 17-
November 4, 1814

Kings of Sweden and Norway 1814-1905

Carl XIII	1814-1818
Carl Johan (Bernadotte)	1818-1844
Oscar I	1844-1859
Carl XV	1859-1872
Oscar II	1872-1905

Kings of Norway since 1905

| Haakon VII | 1905-1957 |
| Olav V | 1957- |

A Culinary Interlude

A CULINARY INTERLUDE

THE RUMOR that Norwegians eat too much is partly based on the fact that they do eat too much; and when they eat, they are in a hurry, probably to stow away as much as possible before the next meal is placed on the table.

If by any chance a foreigner, in the course of a conversation with a Norwegian lady, should happen to touch upon national food specialties, he should not feel disturbed by expressions such as *fårikål, rømmegrøt, torsk* or *lutefisk*. In Sweden he is likely to run into still stranger words like *Janson's frestelse and kaaldolmar*, and in Denmark *tilslørede bondepiger*, all of which, regardless of their Scandinavian origin, describe some of the most cherished edible delights of the people.

The *lutefisk* in particular is rather unique . . . and controversial. Anti-*lutefisk* groups strongly maintain that this dish must have been among the chief reasons that the Vikings left Norway; others suspect it must more likely have been the Hardanger fiddle, or the complicated Norwegian language situation. If these groups are right, they should be reminded then that the discovery of America should also be credited to the *lutefisk*. *Lutefisk* connoisseurs do not readily forgive those statements which the opposing forces have issued, such as: ". . . inedible, a Norwegian horror, a Yuletide atrocity, a taste that can only be experienced and not described, painfully embarrassing to

Norwegians, not adaptable to casual conversation, un-
savorable, weird concoction, hard on the nerves, a night-
mare, a mess you would not set in front of your worst
enemy, now it is there and now it isn't, lutefisk and other
perversions." etc., etc. In short, these opponents do not
at all understand the significance of a *lutefisk* dinner
during the winter season. The proponents of *lutefisk,* who
consider it one of the finest delicacies ever known to mankind, even go one step further and compare it with *gammelost* (old cheese), another highlight of Norse culinary folklore, which supposedly contributed to the victory of King
Harald Fair-haired at the battle of Hafrsfjord in the year
872, which in turn led to a united Norway, his marriage
to Princess Gyda, and his first haircut, whereby he left the
ranks of the hippies of those early Viking times. The saga
writer Snorri Sturluson, as well as other sources, imply
that the King fed his warriors *gammelost* for lunch prior to
the battle, thereby turning them into berserkers. That did
it. The enemy kings fled to their homes where they probably asked their local queens why they hadn't been served
something stronger for breakfast than *blodpølse* (blood
sausage), a third national specialty. This really would have
curled the hair of anyone opposed to *lutefisk*. Like anything Norwegian, *gammelost* is able to walk all by itself
after a certain span of time. As for the *lutefisk,* the
world's largest processor is located in Minneapolis, Minnesota and during a three months' period, has sold more
than one million pounds of it. To the tune of "Oh Su-
sanna" a lyrical-minded *lutefisk* fan once wrote:

>   "Oh, I came to Minnesota
>   With a *jente* on my knee.
>   And some day, I pray, we both
>   Will have *lutefisk* for three!"

Contrary to general belief the Norwegians are not the

world's champions in coffee consumption. This honor goes
to the Swedes who manage to swallow about twenty-one
pounds per capita, as against merely seventeen pounds per
capita in Norway. This figure places Norway on the bottom of the ranking list for all five Nordic nations: Denmark, Finland, Iceland, Norway and Sweden. As for tea,
all of the Scandinavians are way down on the world statistics, but Norwegians seem to enjoy their cocoa as they
lead their Nordic sister nations with 2.3 pounds per capita.

The Norwegian *koldt bord* (cold table) is basically not
too different from the Swedish-inspired *smorgasbord,* the
latter being equipped with selected hot dishes. But whether
it is *koldt bord* or *smorgasbord,* would anyone really care
when he approaches a long table sagging under the massed
abundance at any first-rate Norwegian hotel or restaurant?
He will probably find tempting delicacies (not necessarily
in this order) as follows:

    Herring in any form
    Tossed salad and relish bowls
    Seafood salad
    Fish, rice in curry
    Ham salad
    Potato salad
    Cole slaw
    Sliced cold ham, lamb, beef
    Meat loaves
    Head cheese, tongue, corned beef
    Pickles, cranberries, apple sauce, spiced apples
    Norwegian goat cheese *(geitost)*
    Strong cheese *(gammelost)*
    Blue cheese
    Swiss cheese
    Tyttebär (cowberries)
    Orange marmalade

Apple marmalade
Sardines
Fish pudding
Fish cakes
Pork sausages
Liver loaf
Sylte (from pigs)
Salami
Koteletter
Various bread types (including flatbread)

If by some chance hot dishes are served on the side, then the whole meal turns into a fullfledged culinary orgy, which requires a ritual supervised by the mastermind behind these caloric excesses, the *maitre d'hotel*. These stern guardians of prescribed rules and regulations are not to be ignored. They often provide each customer with a pamphlet entitled "Advice on How Best to Enjoy Your Smorgasbord." In the opinion of people who have pledged allegiance to the frugal things in life, such a publication might be labeled sheer propaganda. In the eyes of pursuers of true palatable pleasures, it is strictly a guide to better living and to permanent happiness on a year-round basis.

One need not be a Rembrandt or a Rubens to relish the roquefort, *rømmegrøt* or rice in curry; but as the pamphlets point out, one should fill one's plate as an artist prepares his palette. In other more prosaic words, don't put everything from the seafood salad through the beef stroganoff to the raisin bread and goat cheese on one single plate. If you insist on gathering up sardines, sliced ham, meat balls, jello, cake, and *gammelost* in one all-encompassing sweep, please don't carry the collection past the *maitre d'hotel*. We have seen strong gastronomic experts break down in tears at the sight of such violations of common *smorgasbord* sense and etiquette. Rather, scan

the pamphlet for advice: "First help yourself to the tossed
salads and other appetizers. Return for cold meats. Then
select from any or all of the hot dishes. Leave room for
the special desserts and top it off with cheeses." This is
the true smorgasbord strategy, the one and only way to
be in command of the situation as it develops around the
table. At the same time you will be heartened to know
that you have saved the *maitre d'hotel* from another sleep-
less night.

Admittedly, rules are easily broken and more so when
the temptation of apple cakes with whipped cream blocks
one's way to the meat loaves or corned beef, which, according to the *maitre d'hotel* have a decisive priority. You
may cover up the cakes with a layer of salad and sneak
past the stern guardian of accepted regulations for the
proper enjoyment of the smorgasbord, or you may be
caught in the act, as once happened to us.

—What's that, may I ask?

—That is your delicious herring salad.

—Never mind the herring salad. What do I spot under
it? It couldn't be apple cake with whipped cream, could it?

—It shouldn't be, but it is. We apologize. We must have
confused it with the apple sauce for the sliced lamb. Please
don't blacklist us or report it to the A.P.B.C.S. (Association of Properly Behaving Customers of *Smorgasbords*).

We are happy to announce that we have since lived up
to the accepted standards. Well maybe once or twice we
have taken the lemon pudding ahead of the fish balls,
but this we understand is a minor offense in the eyes of
the A.P.B.C.S.

Norwegian *Akevitt* (aquavit) is truly the national bev-
erage, a very potent liquor made from potatoes and fla-
vored with caraway seeds. The name is of medieval origin. Alchemists, in their search for gold, discovered a

process of distilling liquor around 1200, and the product was called aqua vita, meaning "water of life." One would think that the Indians of North America saw the facts of the matter more clearly than the medieval alchemists, for their term "fire water" is definitely more realistic.

The finest brand is called "Linje Akevitt." It has been stored in huge sherry vats of oak, made from the New Orleans oak or the American white oak. The lumber is sent by cargo ship. Supposedly the change of climate when crossing the "Line" (Equator) adds a striking flavor to the *akevitt*. It is used mainly with food and entails much "skoaling." The bottle must be cold enough to produce a frosty dew, and the glass should be small enough to make it impossible for the "dram" to become lukewarm before it is consumed.

On its way "down the hatch" the aquavit should be immediately chased by a beer.

Whenever *akevitt* is served at parties in Norway, one must "skoal" *(Skål)*. First find a victim, then raise your glass, look firmly into his eyes and say "skoal." He will do likewise, and then you both drink simultaneously. Finally you both lower your glass at breast level and nod your head. This completes the ceremony. Then you look around for your next victim. Remember, you are never allowed to say skoal to your hostess.

When attending informal parties in Norway, American visitors are sometimes surprised to see the merriment which surrounds the drinking of *akevitt*. On occasion, one must sing before he drinks, and here is the text:

> *Helan går!*
> *Syng hopp fallerallala!*
> *Helan går!*
> *Syng hopp fallerallala!*

Og den som ikke helan tar,
han heller ikke halvan får!
Helan går!

Hell-and gore
Sing hopp fahl-er-alla-lah!
Hell-and gore!
Sing hopp fahl-er-alla-lah!
Aw den som ikkeh hell-an-tahr,
hahn hell-er ikkeh hahl-an fawr!
Hell-and gore!

This is sung before the first dram. Before the second dram, it's *"halvan" går,* and then follows *"tersen," "kvarten"* and *"kvinten."*

For the reader who has already sampled the national delicacies in Norway or in Norwegian America, and no less for the adventuresome reader who has yet to partake in this experience, some of the more memorable recipes have been included in this volume.

*FÅRIKÅL
(Mutton and Cabbage)

2 pounds mutton
2 pounds cabbage
1 head Savoy cabbage
3 cups boiling water
2 teaspoons salt
10 black peppercorns
1 tablespoon chopped parsley

Wash meat and cut in pieces. Parboil cabbage and slice. Arrange meat and cabbage in layers, fat pieces in bottom of saucepan and sprinkle with salt. Tie peppercorns in small piece of cheese cloth and boil with meat. Let simmer under tight lid 2 hours, add Savoy cabbage cut in slices and cook ½ hour more. Sprinkle with parsley and serve. Gourmets prefer this dish when warmed up 3 times. Remember piping hot plates for each serving. Serves 6.

**LAPSKAUS
(Stew)

1 pound fresh beef
1 pound fresh pork or ½ pound salt pork
1 medium sized onion
4 raw potatoes, diced
salt and pepper

Dice meat. Cover with water. Simmer 1 hour. When tender, add diced onion and potatoes. Season to taste. Cook until vegetables are done and stew is thickened. Carrots may be added.

*KÅLRULETTER - FYLT BLOMKÅL
(Stuffed Cauliflower)

1 large, firm cauliflower
1 pound meat, finely minced
2 tomatoes
parsley

Cover bottom of oblong, well-greased baking dish with ½ pound minced meat. Parboil cauliflower 3 minutes in water with small amount of salt. Cut in small bouquets. Put on top of meat. Add remaining meat and steam 1 hour. Turn out on hot serving dish. Decorate with cauliflower flowerets, tomatoes and parsley. Serve with rich brown gravy or tomato sauce. Serves 4.

**KJØTTKAKER
(Meat Balls)

1 pound sirloin steak (ground)
⅓ cup chopped onions
1 teaspoon salt

½ teaspoon pepper
1 tablespoon butter
3 tablespoons milk
2 eggs
butter for frying
½ cup cracker crumbs

Sauté onions in butter until tender, but not brown. Mix with ground sirloin, salt and pepper. Beat yolks and milk together and add crackers. Add to meat mixture. Form into balls and fry in butter. Serves 6.

*RØMMEGRØT
(Cream Porridge)

2 cups thick sour cream
2 quarts milk
1 cup flour
½ teaspoon salt

Boil cream for 5 minutes. Sprinkle in 4 tablespoons flour, beat porridge until butter oozes out. Skim off butter with a silver spoon and keep hot. Add rest of flour, pour on rest of boiling milk. Boil for 5 minutes to a smooth consistency. Add salt. Pour into hot soup plates and pour over a little melted butter. Serve with sugar, cinnamon, and fruit juice, and aquavit for a special occasion. Serves 6.

*KOKT TORSK
(Boiled Cod)

1 large cod (4-5 pounds)
2 pints water
1 cup salt
1 tablespoon vinegar
1 sprig seaweed (optional)

Clean fish without cutting open. Cut into slices. Put under running water, then cover with a few ice cubes.

Bring water, salt and vinegar to a brisk boil. Put in fish, head, liver and roe the minute the water boils and allow to simmer for 4-5 minutes. Skim carefully. In the southern part of Norway it is customary to add a sprig of seaweed to the water. It brings out the fine iodine flavor. Serve fish piping hot with freshly boiled potatoes and softened butter mixed with finely chopped parsley. Mustard, vinegar, pepper and thin rye crisps may accompany this dish. Serves 6.

*LUTEFISK
(Lye fish)

2 pounds lye fish (see below)
4 cups of water
2 ounces salt

Cut fish in large pieces, simmer 1 minute in unsalted water. Add salt and simmer for another 5 minutes. Adding salt after the fish has boiled gives it the right consistency and fine flavor. Serve with freshly boiled potatoes, stewed yellow split peas, melted butter or drippings from roast pork.

Lye fish made of dried cod, is a standing Christmas dish in Norway. Serves 4.

1. Soak fish in water 2 to 3 days. Change water frequently.

2. Skin fish and cure in lye mixture 2 to 3 days (10 quarts water to 2 pints lye).

3. Soak in cold water 2 to 3 days. Change water frequently.

*FERSK KJØTT OG SUPPE
(Fresh Meat and Soup)

3 pounds beef
3 quarts cold water

2 tablespoons salt
2 carrots
1 parsnip
2 leeks
pepper and salt

Sauce:
2 tablespoons butter
1 tablespoon flour
3 cups meat stock
1 tablespoon vinegar
1 tablespoon sugar
2 tablespoons grated horseradish

Wash meat and place in saucepan with cold water. Bring to boil. Skim carefully and allow meat to boil 2 hours. Add clean chopped vegetables, boil for another 30 minutes. Add pepper and salt. Melt butter and flour, add meat stock, simmer for 5 minutes and add seasoning. Serve the soup first. The meat is served as a separate dish, with potatoes and horseradish sauce. This is typical Norwegian-man's fare.

**FISKEKAKER
(Norwegian Codfish Cakes)

1 cup codfish
2 cups potatoes
2 eggs

Soak codfish 2 hours. Drain. Cook fish and potatoes together until done, mash. Add beaten eggs and a little pepper. Form into cakes, fry until brown.

***FATTIGMANN

3 egg yolks
2 whole eggs
4 teaspoons sugar

¼ teaspoon ground cardamon
¼ cup heavy cream
1 tablespoon melted butter
1 teaspoon vanilla
1¼ cups flour (about)

Beat eggs until lemon colored (up to 15 minutes). Combine sugar and cardamon, add gradually to eggs, beating until light. Add butter, cream and vanilla. Gradually stir in flour until dough is just stiff enough to handle. Chill. Roll about ⅓ of dough at a time on floured board until very thin. Cut in 2 inch long strips with fluted wheel or a knife; then cut crosswise at a slant to form a diamond shape. Slit dough at one point of diamond and bring opposite point through the slit. Fry in deep fat at 365° F. about 1 minute or until light brown, turning once. Drain. May be dusted with powdered sugar.

***GORO

3 eggs
1 cup sugar
1 cup heavy cream
2½ cups flour
1 cup melted butter
¼ teaspoon ground cardamon
1 tablespoon brandy or cognac
1 teaspoon vanilla

Beat eggs until lemon colored. Add sugar, beating well. Add remaining ingredients. Roll out like cookies and cut to fit a goro iron. Place cookies in heated iron. Hold over heat, turning until golden brown on both sides. Cut sections while warm.

***KRUMKAKE

1 egg
½ cup sugar
1 cup whipping cream
1¼ cups flour
½ teaspoon baking powder
¼ teaspoon salt
1 teaspoon vanilla

Beat egg well. Add sugar and vanilla. Add whipping cream. Then add the dry ingredients and beat until smooth. When *krumkake* iron is hot on both sides put 1 teaspoon batter on the greased iron and bake over low heat until light brown. Roll on stick immediately, shaping into cones.

LEFSE

8 cups mashed potatoes
½ cup whipping cream, not whipped
8 heaping tablespoons butter
1 tablespoon salt
4 cups flour (scant)

Peel potatoes, cook and then mash with butter, cream and salt. Let them get cold. Mix in flour and roll out rounds of dough paper-thin on lightly-floured board. Bake rounds on grill turning to lightly brown both sides.

An even quicker way to make the lefse is to use instant mashed potatoes. Here is a recipe to make the rounds that way:

POTET LEFSE

1 (7 oz.) package instant potato
2 teaspoons salt
1 tablespoon butter
1 cup rich milk

1 cup boiling water
1 to 1½ cups flour

Place instant potato, salt and butter in mixing bowl. Add boiling water to milk and add the liquid to potato mixture. Mix quickly with wire beater to a thick mashed potato consistency.

Add just enough flour to be able to handle and roll out on floured board. Form into balls and roll very thin. Bake on hot grill, turning to brown both sides.

*EGGNOG VIKING

10 egg yolks
1 whole egg
1 tablespoon water
2 tablespoons white sugar
powdered sugar

Mix all ingredients and whip for 1 hour to a fluffy mixture. Serve immediately in dessert glasses, adding 1 teaspoon brandy per glass. Eggnog Viking is consumed in large quantities on May 17th, Norway's Independence Day. Serves 6.

*MARZIPAN

1 pound ground blanched almonds
3 egg whites
1 pound powdered sugar

Knead sugar, almonds and egg whites into pliant dough. Can be used as sweets, as cakes, or as decorations shaped into flowers or fruit and colored with confectioner's coloring. Marzipan pigs are very popular at Christmas time.

*KRANSEKAKE
(Garland Cake)

1 pound crushed blanched almonds

3 egg whites

1 pound icing sugar

Mix almonds and powdered sugar, adding sufficient quantity of egg white to make mass firm and even. Grease ring-shaped cake forms with butter, press dough through a funnel and place in rings, or squeeze out in even sticks. Bake in slow oven (300° F.) for 20 minutes. Do not remove rings from forms until they are cold. Place rings on top of one another to make a tower or basket. Fasten rings together with caramel sugar, garnish with sugar frosting and decorate with sweets, petit fours and Norwegian flags.

Frosting: Stir together 1 cup powdered sugar, 1 egg white, and 1 teaspoon vinegar. Serves 12.

*OSLO SKOLE FROKOST
(Oslo School Breakfast)

1. 2 cups milk.
2. 1 rusk or a large piece of crispbread, spread with enriched margarine and cheese (usually goat-cheese).
3. Wholemeal bread with cheese or liver paste.
4. From September to May, 1 small tablespoon cod-liver oil.
5. 1 large slice of raw cabbage or ½ an orange or 1 apple.

NORWEGIAN TABLE PRAYERS
Before the Meal

I Jesu navn går vi til bords
Spise og drikke på ditt ord
Deg Gud til äre, oss til gavn
Så får vi mat i Jesu navn. Amen.

We sit down in the name of Jesus,
To eat and drink according to Your Word,

To Your honor, Oh Lord, and for our benefit
We receive food in the name of Jesus. Amen.

After the Meal

I Jesu navn til bords vi satt
Og fikk av Herrens hånd vår mat
Til gavn for legem og for sjel
Gud lat oss det bekomme vel. Amen.

We sat at the table in the name of Jesus,
And received our food from the hand of the Lord
For the benefit of our body and our soul,
May God let it do us much good. Amen.

*From *Norway's Delight* by Elise Sverdrup, published by Johan Grundt Tanums Forlag in Oslo.

**From Sons of Norway Nidaros-Freya Lodge No. 1, Minneapolis, Minn.

***From Norwegian-American Museum, Decorah, Iowa, pamphlet.

Language, Legend and Literature

LANGUAGE, LEGEND AND LITERATURE

THE NORWEGIAN language, together with Danish and Swedish, emerged from the Germanic language group. Anglo-Saxon, the ancestor of modern English, was the Germanic dialect closest to the Scandinavian branch. Today Scandinavians communicate easily with each other in their respective national languages without interpretation. Books, plays, magazines and papers do not require translation and movies need not be dubbed. Quite a few words, however, have a rather different meaning, such as the Swedish *roligt* which means "fun," while in Norwegian it means "quiet" or "peaceful." Thus it is reported that Swedish businessmen have come to Norway, and after completing their work have asked the taxi drivers to take them to a *"roligt"* place and have been promptly delivered to the nearest cemetery! The Norwegian language developed from the Old Norse of saga times and, still very much alive in Iceland, was for centuries related to the Danish language. This of course was a result of the Danish-Norwegian union (1449-1814), in which Norway was so decisively the weaker partner. After the 1814 separation, the nationalistic Norwegian awakening rapidly influenced the language as well as the literature and was spearheaded by the great poet Henrik Wergeland. The eminent linguist professor Einar Haugen of Harvard University has pointed out the difficulty in his monumental work *Nor-*

wegian-English Dictionary: "the new-found pride of nationality called for a language distinctive of the nation, so that the blot on the national scutcheon might be removed. . . . But four centuries had passed since Norway had had a written language of her own, and in the meanwhile the country had developed a great variety of usage. The rural population had no nationwide language, only a vast variety of local dialects. The nearest approach to a nationwide Norwegian was the speech of the bureaucracy and the bourgeoise, a compromise between Norwegian speech and Danish writing."

Gradually a strange linguistic situation developed. In 1853 the self-taught scholar and author Ivar Aasen created a brand new Norwegian literary language based on a number of dialects from the West-Norway area. He called it *det norske landsmål* (the Norwegian national language), now known as *nynorsk* (New Norwegian). In 1885 this language gained national recognition and was introduced into the schools. The commonly spoken Norwegian had been named *riksmål* by the author Bjørnstjerne Bjørnson, but today it is officially called *bokmål* (Book language). During the last thirty years energetic and consistent attempts have been made to fuse *landsmål* and *bokmål* into *samnorsk* (common or pan-Norwegian). For almost a hundred years the bitter fight between the defenders and supporters of these language versions has been raging and no end to the controversy seems to be in sight. It has been jokingly suggested that today every Norwegian commands at least six languages, five of which are Norwegian! The reader will find a number of useful words and expressions in Norwegian, with English translations, by referring to Appendix C.

The hundreds of thousands of emigrating Norwegians had their own language problems. Those who originated from the same districts tried to the fullest extent possible to settle together. Just to hear the same dialect was a comforting feeling under the strenuous circumstances in strange surroundings. In writing, the immigrants retained what they had learned in school in the Old Country and this soon became outmoded in Norway, a situation which for decades was very much in evidence in the Norwegian language newspapers and periodicals published in the United States. The most pressing problem of the pioneers, however, was to learn English. During the transition period when more and more English words and expressions crept into conversations and letters, the mixed language was partly amusing, partly pathetic. As schools and colleges were founded by the settlers, the new generations acquired formal linguistic education and a "language gap" occurred within families. The elders clung to their background while the young people underwent the "Americanizing" process at an accelerating tempo.

This development was of course not unique for the Norwegian-American communities. Other ethnic groups underwent the same experience, particularly when the trend toward isolationism became rather pronounced after World War I. Many readers of newspapers and other publications in Norwegian and other "foreign" languages continued their subscriptions only on the condition that they be mailed under unidentifiable covers!

Between 1917 and 1947 the ratio of Norwegian services in the Norwegian Lutheran Church dropped from 73.1 percent to less than 3 percent, and in 1946 the "Norwegian" in the name of the Church also was dropped.

Even before this significant and illuminating step had been taken, the largest organization of Americans and Canadians of Norwegian birth or descent had not only changed its name from *Sønner av Norge* to "Sons of Norway" but also had introduced English as the official language of their publication, the *Viking*. At the International Convention of the organization, in Chicago in 1942 when these decisions were made, the President stated, ". . . In our gradual and orderly change from a Norwegian thinking and speaking organization to an all-out American fraternal benefit society, no effort has been made to force the issue of a change in the official language of the Order. Members, local lodges and districts have been given individual rights and opportunity to express themselves in whatever language they choose. . . . Language is only a medium for the expression of thought. When Norwegian ceases to be that medium for the great majority of our people, it becomes necessary to use the language that does. . . . There is a strong demand for a medium by which our people may keep in touch with each other and through which our people may receive from dependable sources information of the part we play in the life of this nation as well as the part we and our kinsfolk in Norway and other lands are taking part in shaping the world of tomorrow."

The Norwegian language press and other guardians of the joint cultural heritage so proudly shared for more than a century, are fully aware of the constantly changing conditions and the need for corresponding adjustments where a "Norway outside Norway" is involved. They do not try to keep alive a national-romantic glow that flickered and died with the last century but rather to adapt the best elements of that era to the moods and trends of our times. The American children and students who today learn about the Norwegian language and Norway at special classes and camps and who visit and evaluate Norway are indeed heirs of a heritage which could and can only be interpreted in their own native language.

This heritage was substantially enriched by the literature dealing with all aspects of the life and progress of the pioneers and their children. The works by Professor Ole E. Rolvaag are generally regarded as the finest examples of this literature, particularly his *Giants in the Earth,* originally written in Norwegian in 1924 and translated into English in 1927. Born in Norway in 1876, Rolvaag became a teacher at St. Olaf College, Northfield, Minnesota where he was instrumental in the formation of the Norwegian-American Historical Association in 1925, at the time of the Centennial of the Norwegian emigration to America. He served as secretary of the organization until his death in 1931.

In Norway the dawn of literature was the *Eddas,* a collection of heroic and other songs written down in the early years of the 13th century. Also of extreme significance to the Norwegian national feeling were the *Sagas of the Kings,* which described the lives of the Norwegian kings to the end of the 12th century. These kings had *skalds* (minstrels) whose assignments were to narrate in short heroic stanzas, called *skaldekvad,* the deeds and exploits of the ruler. These poems, with a terse and dramatic style, reveal a peculiar strength and dignity.

In the year 872 a significant sea battle took place in the Hafrsfjord in the district of Rogaland, near the present-day city of Stavanger. Here King Harald Haarfagre (the Fairhaired), who had vowed he would not cut his hair before he had united Norway into one kingdom, defeated the combined fleet of opposing provincial kings. This is, according to the saga chronicler Snorri Sturluson, how the *skald* (bard) Hornklove described this decisive battle:

> *Hørte du i Havsfjord,*
> *hvor hardt de sloss,*

kongen den aettstore
med Kjotve den rike?
Knarrer kom østfra,
kamplystne,
med gapende hoder
og inn-gravne stavnsmykker.

Ladd var de med holder
og hvite skjold,
vesterlandske spyd
og vaelske sverd.
Berserker brølte
da strid blev budt dem
ulvhedner hylte
og jern klirret.

De fristet den fremdjerve,
som å fly dem lärte,
austmennenes konge,
som bor på Utstein.
Skibene stanste han,
da strid han ventet.
Hugg mot skjold hvinte,
før Haklang falt.

Lei blev av landet
mot Luva å verge
halsdigre høvding:
tok holmen til skjold;
de, som var såret,
seg under setene,
baken stakk de op
i bunnen ned hodet.

På baken lot de blinke
de blanke skjold,

de sindige sveiner,
når stein dem ramte.
Østover ilte de
inn over Jären,
hjem fra Havsfjord,
tenkte på mjød-horn.

The following translation is found in "From the Sagas
of Norse Kings," Dreyers Forlag, Oslo, Norway:

Hast thou heard, where yonder,
In Havsfjord, there fought
This king of mighty race
Against Kjotve the Rich?
Ships came from east-way,
All eager for battle,
With grim gaping heads
And rich carved prows.

They carried a load of warriors,
With white shields
And spears from the Westlands
And Welsh wrought swords.
The berserks were roaring
(For this was their battle),
The wolf-coated warriors howling,
And the irons clattering.

They egged on the valiant
King of the Eastmen,
Who taught them to flee,
Who was bider at Utstein;
He stopped the ships
When the strife he expected,
Blows struck on the shields
Ere Haklang was fallen.

Weary of warding
His land from the thick-haired
Was bull-necked King Kjotve
He let the holme shield him
Those who were wounded
Sank under the boards
Upthrowing their buttocks,
Their heads in the bottom.

The cool-headed men
Let the shivering shields
Flash on their backs
When stones were striking them.
Eastward they fled
Home over Jadar
They thought of the mead horns.

During the Middle Ages and well into the 18th century, when Norway was relegated to a secondary position in the Nordic political structure, the national literature was by and large confined to visionary poems and ballads, and folk songs and fairy tales with clear imprints of native traditions and customs. Today these poems and fairy tales, however naive, constitute an important part of a cherished national heritage.

The following folk song from these times came from the village of Vågå in the Gudbrandsdalen valley:

Jeg lagde mig så silde sent om en kveld,
jeg visste ei sorrig eller kvide;
da kom der et bud ifra kjaeresten min;
jeg måtte til henne bortride.
Ingen har jeg elsket over henne.

Så ganger jeg op uti høienloft,
som alltid jeg var vant til at gjøre,
der stander de jomfruer alt uti flokk

og kledde min kjaerest døde.
Ingen har jeg elsket over henne.

Så gikk jeg mig ut i den grønne eng,
der hørte jeg de klokker at ringe,
ei annet jeg visste, ei annet jeg fornam,
enn hjertet i stykker vilde springe.
Ingen har jeg elsket over henne.

I laid me down to rest, and the hour it was late,
I nothing knew of pain or aching sorrow;
Then word to me came from my sweetheart so dear,
to hasten to her ere the morrow;
I have no one ever loved so dearly.

Then quickly I sped to her lofty bower,
Where oft 'twas my wont to be faring;
A group of fair maidens surrounded my love,
They her for the grave were preparing.
I have no one ever loved so dearly.

I fled from the room to the meadow green,
The bells in the church tower were tolling,
But nothing I heard, and nothing then knew,
The grief of my heart was past consoling.
I have no one ever loved more dearly.

In reality only one poet and writer with a clear identity emerged from this period. He was a clergyman, Petter Dass (1647-1708), who wrote mainly about the way of life in his native North Norway. His major collection of poems was entitled *Nordlands Trompet* (The Trumpet of Nordland).

Contact with the literature of Europe was reestablished through the writings of Ludvig Holberg (1684-1754), whose moralizing plays, mainly comedies, helped the founding of theaters in Norway as well as in Denmark, where he spent most of his life as a professor of history.

The first literary symbol of the new national spirit born when Norway declared its independence from Denmark at Eidsvoll in May, 1814, was the poet and patriot Henrik Wergeland (1808-1845), who had as his basic ideal national liberty fused with universal ideas. At the age of twenty he wrote his major dramatic poem "The Creation, Man and the Messiah."

The person of the lonely *seterjente,* or chalet girl, who tended the cows high up in the mountains during the whole summer, formed a major part of the literature and folklore. Her loneliness was movingly interpreted in the poem by Jørgen Moe called *Seterjentens Søndag* (The Chalet Girl's Sunday). The words were later set to music by Ole Bull:

"I gaze on the sun, it mounts in the skies;
The hour for mass will be breaking;
Ah, would I were home 'midst all that I prize;
'Mong folks now the churchward path taking!
As soon as the sunlight's up on its way
The notch in the mountain crest yonder;
Then church bells below for worship today,
Ring forth from the tower as I wander.

To open one's book 'tis useless to try;
And psalms out of doors begin singing;
So distant my loft, 'twould seem, here on high,
That tones become poor while they're ringing.
Ah, happy the one whose voice would in song,
With his and the others blending!
God grant that the harvest come before long;
My flock and myself homeward sending."

Alongside the *seterjente* were those invisible—yet very present— creatures who still live in the folk and fairy tales of Norway. There was the beautiful *hulder* with the emotions of a human but burdened with a cow's tail. Only if she managed to marry a man in church could she free herself from the tail and become fully human. As a result, these creatures constantly chased men. Then there was the *nisse,* a little old and kind man living on the farm. The farmer found it expedient to be on good terms with him and see to it that he was treated well, particularly during Christmas. The tiny *nisse* had wooden shoes, a white beard and a tall pointed red cap. Then there were the *fossegrimen* and *nøkken,* both living in the rivers. The *fossegrimen* was an excellent music teacher, specializing in instruction in the national instrument, the Hardanger fiddle. One had to go to a waterfall on three successive Thursday nights, throw a leg of cured mutton into the water each time, and then the *fossegrimen* would appear and start playing. In the mountain lakes resided the *nøkken,* a less friendly creature who could change into many appearances, such as a white horse. He lured boys and young men into the cold water and claimed them forever. The *hulder* people were everywhere and were believed to steal babies before they were christened. To keep them away it was the custom to put something made of steel in the cradle and the baby's clothes on the way to church. Steel and fire were also used to frighten the *hulder* people away from the chalets when the farmer returned in spring to take over after the underground-beings had resided there during the winter.

Above all, there were the trolls, huge and grotesque, tremendously strong, yet stupid enough to be outsmarted by almost anybody, most easily by the Aladdin of the Norse folk and fairy tales—the boy Askeladden. (For one of the better known Askeladden stories see Appendix D.) The trolls had two and often three heads, but only one eye which they could take out once in awhile to polish. They took turns in using the eye, for which each head conveniently enough had a hole available. For walking canes the trolls used giant trees turned upside down so they could use the roots as handles. If exposed to sunlight, the trolls exploded. Neither could they stand the sound of church bells and many humans, taken into the mountains by trolls, were saved by the clear ringing of the bells.

These magic creatures of Norwegian folklore came to life in the folk and fairy tales. In many ways the fairy tales are similar to those found throughout the world, once more proving that tales and legends have crossed borderlines of countries as well as continents. In the middle of the nineteenth century two young Norwegian students, Peter Christen Asbjørnsen (1812-1885) and Jørgen Moe (1813-1882), wanted to do what the Grimm brothers had done for German tales. For many years the two friends traveled around in Norway collecting basic material. Small, plain and unassuming pamphlets were published and later combined into the first edition of *Norske Folkeeventyr* (Norwegian Folk Tales). This and subsequent volumes were destined to have a far-reaching effect on the national consciousness, coming as they did in a period of national revival after 1814.

The new nationalism evolved into the post-Wergeland literary period, dominated by Bjørnstjerne Bjørnson (1832-1910) and Henrik Ibsen (1828-1906). Additional authors, such as Alexander Kielland (1849-1906), Jonas Lie (1833-1906), Arne Garborg (1851-1924) and especially Knut Hamsun (1859-1952), contributed to what Norwegians proudly have termed the Golden Age of the national literature.

Bjørnson became a champion of some of the nationalistic ideas of Wergeland and throughout his whole life displayed an all-embracing interest in social and political affairs. In his writings, however, he gradually developed into a modern realist. As a poet he achieved the ultimate recognition by every Norwegian by writing *"Ja, vi elsker dette landet,"* the national anthem. Yet it is Bjørnson's "Psalm II" which has given the richest and fullest expression to the faith of his later years. His poem is perhaps one of the most outstanding ever written in the Norwegian language:

SALME II

Äre det evige forår i livet
Som allting har skapt!
Oppstandelsens morgen det minste er givet.
Kun former går tapt.
Slekt føder slekt,
Stigende evne den når;
Art føder art
I millioner av år.
Verd'ner forgår og oppstår.

Uendelig alt, hvor det
Minste og største
Løper i ett.
Ingen skal skue det siste—
Det første ingen har sett
Ordenens lov
Bärer det alt i sin favn;
Frukt og behov
Føder hverandre, vårt savn
Møter det samledes gavn.

Bland dig i livsfryden, du som fikk väre
Blomst i dens vår.
Nyde et døgn til det eviges äre

I menneskekår.
Yde din skjerv
Inn til det eviges hverv.
Liten og svak
Ånde et eneste drag
Inn av den evige dag.

PSALM II

Hail to the springtime of
Deathless creation,
That all things obey,
Glad in the morning of
Regeneration,
Though forms pass away!
Still they go on.
Win to perfection more near,
Ever new-born,
Out of the earth they uprear
Worlds die and others appear.

Infinite scheme—least and
Greatest united,
Merge into one.
None saw the first,
And the last can be sighted
Surely by none.
Deep-founded law
Labors, the whole to maintain;
Each part will draw
Help in its need, and our pain
Means but that others will gain.

Join in the rapture with spirit undaunted;
Blossom and be!
Cherish the day the Eternal has granted
Man-child, to thee!

Weak as thou art
Grudge not the gift of thy heart!
Heedless of death,
Draw once for all a full breath—
Of the Eternal be part!

Bjørnson, Knut Hamsun and Sigrid Undset (1882-1949) were awarded the Nobel prizes in literature in 1903, 1920 and 1928, respectively.

Henrik Ibsen, introspective and reflective by nature, was a romantic writer in the early stage of his career. Later his writings became more psychological and symbolic and the structure of his plays became a model for playwrights everywhere. Though the form and content of his dramas do have an undimmed appeal and quality, certain characters in the plays have had an impact on contemporary social conflicts and controversies inside Norway. Ibsen constantly stressed the responsibilities of the individual and *Peer Gynt,* published in 1867, is perhaps the strongest case in point.

Today it is a Norwegian national dramatic treasure. This clearly anti-romantic work spoke not only to Ibsen's fellow countrymen at home, but also to Norwegian-Americans. Ibsen hoped that every Norwegian at home and abroad would identify himself, in whole or in part, with Peer Gynt, the symbol of a Norseman at his worst and at his best. While writing *Peer Gynt,* Henrik Ibsen felt keenly his bitterness not only toward the Norwegians but also toward the Swedes for their lukewarm attitude when their sister country, Denmark, was engaged in a bloody war with Germany in 1864. Peer Gynt was a liar, a dreamer, a braggard, a man constantly on the lookout for his own good, who portrays himself this way:

If you could but see my innermost self
You'd find only Peer there, and Peer all through—

Nothing else in the world, no, nor anything more.
Peer, as Ibsen depicted him, was the symbol of inordinate self-love. Yet ironically, the very same Peer Gynt whom Ibsen had painted and held before his fellow Norwegians, saying, "Now take a good look at yourselves, good people," turned into a popular national hero. The Norwegians took it upon themselves to reevaluate Peer Gynt to the extent of glorifying him during World War II.

As an occupied nation the people united over their cultural values as never before, and under these conditions the figure of Peer Gynt assumed certain heroic model proportions in Peer's freeness in speech and deed. Abroad, the part of Peer was played as pure Norwegian propaganda. Since that time *Peer Gynt* has been performed many times in many countries and has been accepted as ". . . not a journey through Norway, but a journey through a man's mind." When all is said and done, *Peer Gynt* is not a reckoning with Norwegians but with each one of us. One hundred years after *Peer Gynt*, Mother Aase, Solveig, Anitra, the Bøygen, the Mountain King, and the Button Molder were created, new sources of light appear from their depths, lights which unexpectedly illuminate our lives. *Peer Gynt* in any country may be recognized as a great imaginative panorama with echoes from the Norwegian folklore. Fridtjof Nansen, the great Norwegian explorer, author, and humanitarian, gave credit for many of his exploits to Peer Gynt. He stated that Peer Gynt kept egging him on to greater achievements. Even the negotiations preceding the dissolution of the Union with Sweden have been traced to the same source.

Aside from Sigrid Undset and Knut Hamsun, whose command of the Norwegian language has been considered unrivaled, very few Norwegian writers of the 20th century have gained true international stature. The literary output of the last few decades has been dominated by the novel and lyrical poetry, and drama has mainly been expressed by the realistic problem play.

Poetry from three eras of Norwegian literary history has been included here: the saga times, the medieval interlude and the "Golden Age." To complete the poetry cycle it would seem appropriate to include a sample from more contemporary times. The poet Nordahl Grieg (1902-1943) was the outstanding voice of Free Norway during World War II until he was killed while participating in a British bombing raid against Berlin. His "17 *mai* 1940" will always be remembered and cherished by his Norwegian compatriots.

17 Mai, 1940

I dag står flaggstangen naken
blant Eidsvolls grønnende traer.
Men nettopp i denne timen
vet vi hva frihet er.
Der stiger en sang over landet,
seirende i sitt språk,
skjønt hvisket med lukkede leber
under de fremmedes åk.

Det fødtes i oss en visshet;
Frihet og liv er ett,
så enkelt så uunnvaerlig
som menneskets åndedrett.
Vi følte da trelldommen truet
at lungene gispet i nød
som i en sunken u-båt . . .
Vi vil ikke dø slik en død.

Verre enn brennende byer
er den krig som ingen kan se,

som legger et giftig slimslør
på bjerker og jord og sne.
Med angiverangst og terror
besmittet de våre hjem.
Vi hadde andre drømmer
og kan ikke glemme dem.

Langsomt ble landet vårt eget
med grøde av hav og jord,
og slitet skapte en ømhet,
en svakhet for liv som gror.
Vi fulgte ikke med tiden,
vi bygde på fred, som i tross,
og de hvis dåd er ruiner
har grunn til å håne oss.

Nu slåss vi for rett til å puste.
Vi vet det må demre en dag
Da nordmenn forenes i samme
Befriede åndedrag.
Vi skiltes fra våre sydpå,
Fra bleke, utslitte menn.
Til dere er gitt et løfte;
At vi skal komme igjen.

Her skal vi minnes de døde
Som gav sitt liv for vår fred.
Soldaten i blod på sneen,
Sjømannen som gikk ned.
Vi er så få her i landet:
Hver fallen er bror og venn.
Vi har de døde med oss
Den dag vi kommer igjen.

May 17, 1940

Naked the flagstaff rises
Through the green of the Eidsvold trees,
But even in this hour of peril
We still know what freedom is.
A song from the land is rising,
With victory's power it grows,
Though whispered by lips tight fastened
Under the gag of our foes.

In us is born the conviction
That freedom is life's first law,
And our faith is as deep and simple
As the very breath we draw.
We felt when tyranny threatened
That our lungs were gasping for breath
As in a sunken U-boat,
We will not die such a death.

Worse than our burning hamlets
Is the war that no one can see,
That spreads its poisonous mantle
Over snowcap and meadow and tree.
With fear of spies and denouncement
They wove their insidious net;
But other dreams we have cherished,
And them we can not forget.

Slowly the land we conquered
With oar and axe and hoe,
And toil made it sweet to live in
And tender for life to grow.
We followed not the new fashion,
On peace we founded our state,
And those whose deeds are destruction
May treat us with scorn and hate.

We fight for the right to breathe now.
The day may still dawn when we,
The Norse folk, may draw in together
The old air of liberty.
We are severed from all to the southward,
From the pale, the worn-out men.
To them we have given our promise
That we shall come back again.

Our dead we here shall remember;
Their lives for our peace they gave;
The soldiers who bled in the snowdrift,
The sailors who sank in the wave.
We are so few in the Northland,
But the dead will be with us then—
Our fallen brothers and neighbors—
The day we come back again.

English translation by G. M. Gathorne-Hardy, "20th
Century Scandinavian Poetry" by Martin Atwood.

Art—Vikingland and Vigeland

ART—VIKINGLAND AND VIGELAND

PREHISTORIC ROCK carvings have been found by the thousands all over Norway. They generally have depicted the hunting and fertility arts, themes on which Norwegian pictorial art has been built through the centuries. The first great period of creative achievements in Norwegian medieval art came with the introduction of Christianity in the 11th century. Thereafter two main strands of the culture were definable: one based essentially on the old native traditions and the other entirely inspired by European trends. Norway at that time had some significance in the over-all European scene but this position was lost in the political, economic and artistic decline of the late Middle Ages. The national art continued to live on among the people and at a later date flourished once more in the Norwegian folk art. Norwegian farmers preserved their individual freedom to a far higher degree than farmers in most European countries. Attempts to feudalize Norway were never fully carried out, nor were the farmers completely impoverished. They benefited greatly from the new prosperity and by the end of the 18th century two thirds owned their own land. Specialized community crafts developed, thus laying the foundation for the revival of folk art. Tapestry weaving, wood carving and rosepainting were the three dominating art forms from 1700 to about 1850. Then the transition from a natural economy based on self-sufficiency, to a modern agricultural society marked by mechanical operation and close intercourse, both materially and culturally, caused a gradual decline in the traditional folk art. In addition, the great emigration waves to the United States swept with them many of the most outstanding and dedicated folk artists in search of a better livelihood. Subsequent attempts to restore the folk art form to the place it once held have had some measure of success, but they have not succeeded in giving it a natural function in the technologically developed Norway of today.

One may safely assume that the first national costume of Norway was the bear or wolf skin. But as civilization developed, the customs and garb of medieval Europe appeared in Norway. These in turn were influenced by the Vikings who returned from their adventures with goods and clothing never before seen in Norway. Gradually the men shed their coats of mail, while the women became evermore color-conscious, particularly along the eastern valleys.

Aware of the changing trends abroad, the Norwegians nevertheless knew how to adapt the new styles to make them more suitable for rural life. Thus the styles differed from district to district and from valley to valley. Even today about 150 different folk costumes may be counted, some easily traceable back to European fashions, from the Renaissance, Philip II of Spain, Louis XIV of France and other royal pacesetters. Eventually a national Norwegian style did emerge, with closefitting breeches, silver and pewter buttons, long tail coats and contrasting colors.

Today the national costumes or *bunader* are proudly worn by tens of thousands of women and also by many men, mainly on May 17th, but also at many other public and private events. Most famous abroad of all these *bunader* is the so-called *Hardangerdrakt,* with its marvelous embroidery — white on white, black on white and beads embroidered on scarlet cloth. Featured on travel posters and promotional multicolored pamphlets, the *Hardangerdrakt* has more or less become a national symbol in line with the stave church, the Viking ships and the midnight sun.

The same beautiful designs worked without a traced pattern on fine linen are found in many other regions. Of the male costumes, the Telemark costume is regarded as the finest and most distinguished one: black and white with black embroidery on the white cloth. The women's dresses are set off by silver brooches and clasps, and both men and women wear buckled shoes. Brides used to wear a silver bridal crown, exchanging this on the second day after the wedding for the *skaut* (kerchief) of the married women.

The great eras of Norwegian pictorial art were the early Middle Ages (1100-1350) and the last century. The oldest paintings still in existence are a group of painted altar fronts from the 13th century which command international interest as being among the first known examples of oil painting. A number of sculptures of a still earlier date have also been preserved.

During the Danish domination, with the exception of the folk arts, independent artistic activity and achievement came almost to a standstill. Most artists were foreigners, mainly Dutch and German painters, wood-carvers and decorators of churches. Even following the 1814 acts of independence the pictorial artists were comparatively slow in coming into their own as contributors to the national revival.

The major turning point came with the first great landscape painter Johan Christian Dahl (1788-1857) who

was succeeded by several painters of the Romantic period;
Thomas Fearnley (1802-1842), Hans Gude (1825-1903),
and Adolph Tiedemand (1814-1876). Later artists advocated naturalism and impressionism: Erik Werenskiold
(1855-1938), who illustrated Snorri Sturluson's *Sagas of
the Kings;* Theodor Kittilsen (1857-1914), Norway's most
popular illustrator of fairy and folk tales; Harriet Backer
(1845-1932), Norway's most prominent woman painter
and Christian Krohg (1852-1935). A copy of his famous
painting "Leiv Eiriksson Discovers America" hangs in the
Capitol in Washington, D. C.

A highly personal art based on modern expressionism
was introduced by Edvard Munch (1863-1944), whose
genius overshadowed and dominated Norwegian painting
at the turn of the century. His epoch-making works are
found mainly in the Edvard Munch museum in Oslo and
the new Henie-Onstad Cultural Center near Oslo which
was established by the late skating queen Sonja Henie and
her husband, shipowner N. Onstad.

In the field of sculpture Gustav Vigeland (1869-1943)
stands almost alone in terms of international fame. He produced an unbelievable number of great works. One hundred fifty groups have been assembled at the Vigeland
Park in Oslo, capped by the huge Fountain of Life and
the giant fifty-three foot high Monolith. Vigeland carried
on the thirty thousand year development of the human
figure in art and he added to this tradition. His work has
further enlarged the scope of humanistic art in all of its
healthy and natural relationships. The American sculptor,
Nathan Cabot Hale, calls Vigeland's work a new art form:
"It is an art for new men who must be equipped to understand the laws of nature as science reveals the cosmos.
But it is also an art for men who must understand their
innermost selves and the laws of nature that operate in

the re-creation of life. Vigeland's work will prevail and tell mankind of his place in nature."

Norway has pioneered the way to make art and art forms available to the people. In all sections of manufacturing industries art pieces are brought from the museums and galleries to the canteens and assembly halls of the factories. Prominent artists have also been commissioned to decorate and enhance the interiors as well as the surrounding areas of the industrial concerns. Edvard Munch, Norway's most famous painter, was engaged to decorate the walls in the country's largest candy factory.

The society *Kunst på Arbeidsplassen* (Art in the Workshop), formed in 1950, stresses four basic aims: to bring beauty and congenial atmosphere to places where people work; to spread an understanding of art; to develop this understanding through lectures by experts during the lunch hour periods, and, through art, to bring people closer together by arranging congenial social gatherings in connection with the exhibits of originals and prints.

All pictures exhibited are owned by the Society, which buys them directly from the artists or from the galleries in Europe and America. The works are placed in mats of four standard sizes and accompanied with literature, a guide, slides and filmstrips. At each place, the displays are changed three or four times a year. After a few weeks the exhibit is explained by an artist or historian, either at a prolonged lunch-break or in the evening, followed by discussions and poetry reading or a music program.

The Society is headed by a board representing the Employers' Organization, the trade unions and art experts. Extensive support has been rendered by the state and municipalities. Experimental performances by theater ensembles at the factories have also brought rewarding results.

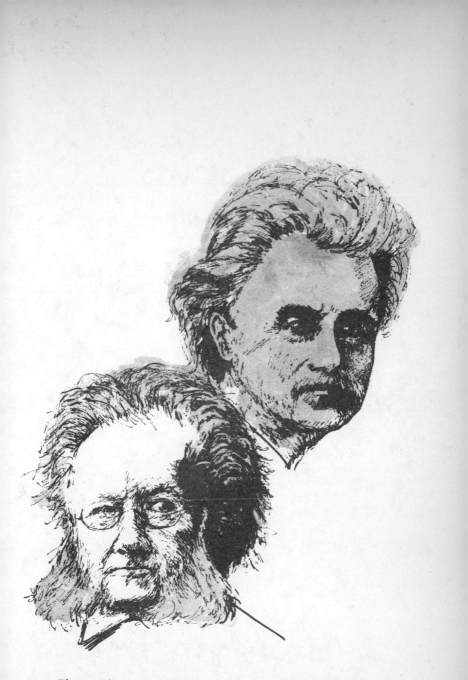

They Blew A Horn . . . And Anitra Danced

THEY BLEW A HORN . . . AND ANITRA DANCED

EVIDENCE exists that the early Vikings had not only drinking horns, but also horns to blow. Of about thirty horns from the Bronze Age, two have been found in Norway, which was, by and large, the last area to emerge from the Ice Age. It may also be assumed that the Scandinavian peoples knew some kind of harmony, in a musical sense, at that early stage of history. From then on, nearly all music produced in Norway up to the 19th century was anonymous folk music. These songs and dances, never written down, had a greater importance in Norway than in other European countries. When Norwegian music finally evolved into the classical art-form, the composers adopted the classical forms of the sonata, the concerto and the symphony to the material provided by folk, ballad and dance tunes. Norwegian Christian church music also developed independently and many of the ballads, such as the greatest folk poem of them all, *Draumkvedet* (Vision of Heaven and Hell), had religious themes. Together with the hymns these were the most significant elements of Norwegian folk music. Among the most beautiful folk tunes, recorded on paper for the first time in the 1800's, was *"Astri, mi Astri."*

> *Astri, mi Astri som eine helt tå meg,*
> *Den ti' eg var deg så inderlig god,*
> *Den ti' du gret ko hver gang eg gik fra deg,*

Som du hver einaste laurdagskveld såg.
Ja den ti' da va' eg den gjevaste gut,
Inkje eg bytte me Prest eller Fut.

Out of the past, now when shadows are falling
Soundly resound happy memories of you,
Often in dreams I can hear someone calling,
Whispering softly "I love you, I do"
How well I remember those days long ago,
You were my sweetheart and I was your beau.

Another extremely popular folk song expressing a solid
sense of humor was *Pål sine Honer* (Paul On the Hillside):

Paul let his chickens run out on the hillside,
Over the hill they went tripping along;
Paul understood by the way they were acting;
Feeling a warning that something was wrong:
Cluck, cluck, cluck, The chickens were cackling;
Paul was aware of the task he was tackling:
"Now I'm afraid to go home to my ma!"

The most popular of all these tunes, sung and danced
particularly at Christmas around the Christmas tree, is
Kjerringa me' staven (Limping Down the Valley):

Kjerringa me' staven,
Høgt op i Hakkedalen,
Otte potter rømme, fire merker smør;
Sa kjinna Kari, Ole hadde før,
Kjerringa me' staven.

Kjerringa me' kjeppen,
Hoppa så over bekken;
Vil du vera kjerring, skal je' vera mand,
Vil du koke kaffi, skal je' bera vand,
Kjerringa me' kjeppen.

Limping down the valley,

Cane in her hand came Sally;
Half a pound of butter, to the quart of cream;
That was Sally's churning, She was Ole's dream
Limping down the valley.

Sal' with cane so crooked,
Jump'd clear across the brooklet;
If you'll be my sweetheart, I'll be your man;
If you'll cook the coffee, I'll fill the can,
Limping down the valley.

The centuries old dances such as the *springar* (spring-dance) and *gangar* (walk-dance) later became parts of works by Edvard Grieg and Johan Svendsen and the music for these dances came mainly from the ultra-Norwegian national instrument, the *hardingfele,* the Hardanger fiddle. This instrument has four sympathetic strings under the usual four strings. The sounds of this strange instrument are very frequently imitated in Edvard Grieg's piano pieces. But the ordinary violin became the instrument of one of Norway's most noted and internationally known artists— Ole Bull (1810-1880)—who toured extensively in Europe and America. His fame rests not only on his magical ability to move an audience but also on his own personality, vitality and flair for publicity.

Richard Nordraak (1842-1866), whose own compositions reveal strength and a rich sensuality, is best remembered as the composer of the music for the national anthem, *Ja, vi elsker.* He ought to be remembered also for his efforts to develop a national art form.

Richard Nordraak became the inspiration for Edvard Hagerup Grieg (1843-1907), Norway's most famous composer, yet it was the violinist Ole Bull who discovered the potential genius of the young Grieg. One afternoon in 1858, when Ole Bull visited the Grieg family in Bergen, the fifteen year old Edvard extemporized on the piano playing some of his first modest compositions. Ole Bull took the parents aside, discussed his impressions of Edvard's playing, gave his advice, and concluded by telling young Grieg, "You will have to go to Leipzig in order to become an artist." The parents did not even ask for time to consider. Ole Bull was the undisputed king of Norwegian art and his words were a royal decree. Edvard Grieg did go to Leipzig and when he returned from Germany he became inspired by Norwegian folk music and was the first Scandinavian to compose nationalistic music. Among his most internationally known and beloved works are "Concerto in A minor for piano and orchestra," "Norwegian Dances and Folk Songs," the Peer Gynt selections such as "Morning," "Åse's Death," "Anitra's Dance" and "In the Hall of the Mountain King." He also wrote a number of songs, including "A Swan," "Departed," and "I Love Thee." Of his own music Grieg once said, "Artists like Bach and Beethoven erected churches and temples on ethereal heights. My aim in my music is exactly what Ibsen says about his own plays, I want to build homes for people in which they can be happy and contented."

Other Norwegian composers of stature in the past century have been Johan Svendsen (1840-1911), Halfdan Kjerulf (1815-1868), Christian Sinding (1856-1943), Harald Säverud (1897-   ), Klaus Egge (1908-   ), Ludvig Irgens Jensen (1894-   ), Sparre Olsen (1903-   ), and Fartein Valen (1887-   ).

In any discussion about performing musicians of international stature the name of the great opera singer Kirsten Flagstad (1895-1962) comes most easily to mind. Following her brilliant career at the Metropolitan Opera in New York she became the first director of the permanent opera in Oslo.

Permanent theaters in Norway date back only 150 years. The theater in Oslo opened in 1827 and the theater in the second largest city, Bergen, in 1860. By 1899 the first National Theater came into being in Oslo and later other principal cities, such as Trondheim and Stavanger, acquired permanent stages.

It is natural that the Norwegian theater was profoundly influenced by Henrik Ibsen and Bjørnstjerne Bjørnson.

Riksteatret—the State Traveling Theater—was started in 1949 and Norway, with the other Scandinavian countries, became a pioneer in systematically bringing the theater to the people. In rugged Norway, with long rough winters and vast distances to be covered, this task has never been an easy one for the players and stagehands associated with this ambitious project. Yet in one recent season more than 700 performances were given in spite of all the physical difficulties and adverse conditions.

Plays presented over the years which have attracted at least 80 percent of capacity audiences have been *The Diary of Anne Frank, Hamlet, Peer Gynt, Anna Christie, A Doll's House* and *Candida*. The noted Israeli producer and theater manager Joseph Milo, after traveling in Norway and seeing some of the performances by the *Riksteatret,* stated, "On my theater journey in Europe I have been searching for the pioneer spirit that is essential at home. I have found it here!"

The *Riksteatret* maintains a rich repertoire of classical and modern plays, but its range also extends to light comedies. In addition to being financially a state supported activity, much of its subsidy also comes from the soccer pools which have become an important part of the Norwegian social structure. Most of the money from these sources is used for building community halls with suitable stages.

While permanently employed actors are engaged on a twelve-month contract, talent is also drawn from other theaters as well as from radio and television, all in the spirit of Hamlet's advice, ". . . let them (the players) be well used; for they are the abstracts and brief chronicles of the time . . ."

"S" Stands for Sports

"S" STANDS FOR SPORTS

THE MOST popular sports activities in Norway seem to start with an "S"—skiing, skating, sledding, sailing, swimming, soccer, and, on occasion in the grandstands when everything goes well for the national colors, particularly while downing the Swedes in soccer matches, skoaling.

Skiing, above all, is *the* national sport and pastime. Before weekends and winter vacations, the conversational question is not are you going skiing, but where. At Easter time the very successful "Know the Norwegians" program of the travel promoters must be interrupted because nobody is home in Norway. A foreigner has almost the whole capital city of Oslo to himself. The long building facades echo the hollow loneliness of his walk along empty streets, normally bustling with traffic. The natives have all gone over the hills. The foreigner may continue living his winter version of a Robinson Crusoe existence, or he may round up a pair of skis and poles and set out after the Norwegians, to share their sundrenched happiness while their skis carry them across mountains and meadows, through deep forests silenced by the snow, and down the slopes.

How long has this been going on? Saga writer Snorri Sturluson described the Norse Viking kings of the 9th and 10th centuries as very good skiers. Historians have examined rock carvings which date back five thousand years, in and outside caves all over the country. They reveal

runners resembling modern skis, indicating that prehistoric Norwegians were acquainted with this means of transportation. The skis must have served them well in quite a
few situations, such as a fast flight from any roaming mas-
todon or polar bear, or for more romantic purposes. No
wonder the myth about Norwegians being born with skis
emerged so early and has persisted so long.

During a war in the year 1206 the two year old Crown
Prince Haakon Haakonson was saved from falling into
enemy hands by the quick action of two of the fastest
skiers of that time, Torstein Skevla and Skjervald Skrukke.
On skis, they carried the child across the mountains of
central Norway. They belonged to the King's special guard
called "Birch Legs," and today there is an annual ski race
covering 35 miles called the "Birch Leg Ski Race" to commemorate this great feat.

The first modern skiing competition took place in the
middle of the 18th century, and in 1861 the world's first
ski club was formed with the name of Trysil Shooting and
Skiing Club. Contests have since been held in the form of
cross-country races, slalom (one of many Norwegian contributions to international ski terminology), down-hill, a
number of combinations of these varieties, and finally,
ski jumping, the only suicidal attempt not included in the
book by Dr. G. Hendin, *Suicide in Scandinavia*. In 1879
the first big ski jumping contest took place near Oslo,
with 10,000 spectators. The Ski Promotion Society was
founded in Oslo in 1883 and has since organized every
major contest and exhibit, designed skis and presented skis
to school children. This society formed the Norwegian Ski
Association in 1908 which in turn was instrumental in
founding the International Ski Association in 1910.

Basically ski jumping follows rather simple rules: The
contestant climbs or is lifted to the top of a tower where

he has a commanding view of a sizeable section of the land. A narrow slide, called the inrun, leads way down to a protruding point—the take-off or lip—a distance traveled with a speed accelerating up to 100 m.p.h. At this stage of the game the jumper is transformed into a bird-like creature. His whole body is stretched up and forward to the utmost as he seemingly tries to brush the ski tip with his tongue. Arms are held closely to his hips and the two skis look more like one solid plank of wood. The length of the ride through the air is determined by the ability of the jumper and the size of the hill. When he finally is reunited with terra firma to the accompaniment of a resounding bang and thunderous applause by expert onlookers, he starts his long way up the hill for a second try at the hill record and the top prize. This scene is repeated Sunday after Sunday all over Norway until the climactic event of the season: The Holmenkollen Meet.

The Holmenkollen ski jumping hill—Mecca of competing jumpers all over the world—can easily be seen looming against the Oslo horizon from almost any point in the Norwegian capital city. For close to 80 years Holmenkollen has been a magnet for millions of spectators from all parts of Norway and abroad. The jumping contest is but one event of a week-long series covering all aspects of skiing, yet the spectacular sight of champions soaring through the exhilarating air is without doubt the most exciting and fascinating one of all. In his youth the present King of Norway, Olav V, also participated in the contest and was a prize winner. Everybody gathers at Holmenkollen, from the Royal Family and their guests to the world-famous *bikja i unnarennet* (the dog on the landing slope) which always appears from nowhere and is hotly pursued by the meet officials and their assistants while the vastly amused audience of 100,000 roars its approval.

Whether they are encouraging the dog or the chasers is a rather difficult question to settle. The winner of the meet is truly the King of the Hill. It is a triumph fought for and cherished as much as any other national or international championship, including the Olympics, which also have frequently been won by Norwegians since 1924 when the first Winter Olympics were held.

Most winter tourists coming to Norway do not generally head for the jumping hills, but are more apt to settle for the long, inviting slopes close to famous winter resorts, with ski lifts, organized ski schools and a happy apres-ski atmosphere. They know they are in the country with the "cradle of skiing." Perhaps they do not know that the Norwegians introduced skiing to America during the great emigration wave westward, to Australia in 1855, to New Zealand in 1857 and to South America in 1890. Norwegian gold diggers went to Alaska on skis in 1896. A Norwegian missionary skied in China, and in 1902 the Norwegian Consul in Kobe amazed the Japanese with his skiing. Norwegians were also the first to ski in Africa and on Continental Europe. When the young scientist, humanitarian and statesman Dr. Fridtjof Nansen crossed the icefields of Greenland on his skis in 1888, he contributed considerably to the popularization of cross-country skiing in several countries as his books were translated into many languages. Between 1893 and 1896 he sailed in the ship "Fram" to reach the North Pole. Locked in the pack ice, he and companion Hjalmar Johansen left the ship and skied towards the Pole. They spent over four months on this trek and reached the point of 86° 14', when they were forced to return. Another Norwegian explorer, Roald Amundsen, set out for the South Pole on skis in 1911 and after 99 days he and his fellow-Norwegians planted the Norwegian flag on the southernmost point of the world. This feat, too, increased the general interest in cross-country skiing, not only in Norway but throughout the world.

As Norwegian skis have conquered the world a number of Norwegian ski expressions and terms have been included in many languages. The word "ski" itself is Norwegian as is "slalom" ("sla" means a slope, "lom" a trail). "Telemark" is a method of braking by swinging, perfected by the farmers in the Province of Telemark in the 1870's, and "Christiania" or just "Christi," another turning method, was named after the capital city before it was rechristened Oslo.

For several years the most unique ski race in the world —called the Knight's Race— has been staged at Beitostølen in the district of Valdres in central Norway. The race is exclusively for the blind and near-blind, as well as the physically handicapped men and women from all around the world. There is a cross-country race covering a distance of about 35 miles where the racers use deep trails and are escorted by famous Norwegian skiers and noted personalities from every walk of life. The program also includes relay skiing, dogsled driving and ice sled pushing. The long-range plan is to create a health sports center at Beitostølen, a project in which the Lions Clubs have been particularly interested and which will be the first one of its kind in the world.

Emigrating Norwegians, mainly those coming to America, brought their skis with them as part of their luggage and became pioneers in a field which today provides recreational enjoyment for millions of Americans. They formed ski clubs in the United States as early as the 1880's and became the prime force behind the founding of the National Ski Association at Ishpeming, Michigan, where the National Ski Hall of Fame and Museum is located. Most remarkable skier of them all was Sondre Norheim from Telemark, Norway, who is called the Father of Modern Skiing. He settled in North Dakota and died there in 1897.

Destined to become most famous of all Norwegian-American skiers, however, was John Thoresen Rue, better known as "Snowshoe" Thompson, who became a legendary figure in his own lifetime. Also born in Telemark, in 1827, Thompson was smitten by the gold fever and went westward where there was a demand for mail service to the isolated settlements east of the Sierra Nevadas and a need for overland communication between San Francisco and the east by way of Salt Lake City. For twenty years Thompson carried the mail alone between California and Nevada, a distance of 90 miles across the high and rugged mountains on his "snowshoes," which in reality were a pair of home-made Norwegian skis. The bags he carried often weighed 80 or 90 pounds. He traveled by night as well as by day; he knew the position of the stars and set his course by them. He kept the line of communication open without a contract, delivering mail which otherwise would not have reached California during winter. He never got paid and in 1876 he died, only 49 years old. A State Park in California today carries his name.

Now we turn to the other favored great S-sport of winter-Norway: skating. Frozen bays, lakes, rivers and rinks are fairly teeming with skaters of all ages and sizes. Some skate for the sheer fun of it, some inspired by the aces of yesterday and today who became in rapid succession Norwegian, European, World and Olympic champions. Others try to live up to the all-time idol of figure skating, Sonja Henie . . . ten times World Champion and three times Olympic Champion. From skating star to movie star she recorded her story for fellow countrymen aspiring to similar championships in a book entitled *Wings on My Feet*. It is a good manual from which to learn figure skating if one only can get the knack of it: ". . . Your first move will undoubtedly be a spiral." Immediately the novice will become aware that Miss Henie knew what she was talking about. He does a spiral. He might even at this early stage manage to combine five or six lessons into one, while executing what the Queen of the Ice termed: ". . . a free foot swing in a slight arc from front to back, with right angles to the heel with continuous rise and fall of the skating knee. . . ." In the process, he might also accomplish in one single move all the compulsory and free skating tests according to the U. S. Figure Skating Association: double threes, loops, counters, rockers, brackets, jumps, spins and splits . . .

If indeed he does survive his first figure skating lesson, the novice might turn to bobsledding, tobogganing, or, if so inclined, simply ice fishing.

Dogsled racing was the national sport in the heyday of early Alaska. The All-Alaska Sweepstakes—more than 400 miles run through rugged terrain in bitter winter cold —were the races that really counted. Three times they were won by a Norwegian immigrant, Leonard Seppala, who arrived in Alaska from Skjervøy, Norway, in 1900. The purse of the Sweepstakes at times reached $10,000, and in 1915 Seppala won it with a time of 76 hours, driving a team of Siberian dogs. In addition to the Alaska races, he also won some 30 other races in the U. S. and Canada, the longest run being 120 miles which he covered in 18 hours. Seppala was generally recognized as the "King of the Trail." His greatest achievement came in 1925 when Nome, Alaska, was struck by an epidemic of diptheria which quickly exhausted the supply of serum at the local hospital. It could only be replenished by serum from Fairbanks, 600 miles away, and the only way to get it would be by dog team and sled. The run was set up in relays with Seppala covering the first leg from Nome, while another Norwegian, Einar Kaasen, set out from Fairbanks. Seppala met one of the other drivers and started the return trek to Nome, covering altogether 268 miles in a fierce arctic blizzard. Seppala's lead dog Togo was mounted after his death and is now on exhibit at Yale University.

When Admiral Richard E. Byrd made his trip to the South Pole in 1928, Seppala was selected to come along to direct the work of placing markers in the icebound wastes which would guide the pilots to their landing places. He died in Seattle, Washington, in 1967.

During the summer of 1896 two Norwegian-American sailors made "sport" history their own way by rowing across the Atlantic Ocean. Working as clam gatherers along the New Jersey coast, Frank Samuelson, 26, and George Harbo, 30, equipped their 18 foot 4 inch skiff named "Fox" with five pairs of oars, 60 gallons of fresh water and 100 pounds of bread, canned meats and oatmeal which they expected would last through the 3,250 mile distance they expected to cover in 65 days. For navigation they had a compass and a sextant. Leaving Manhattan on June 7 they were off the Newfoundland banks in a month. Huge waves overturned "Fox" but they managed to roll her over on the keel. Stove and food had disappeared. For the next week they fought the mountainous waves and storms in the half swamped boat. They encountered two vessels and were given new supplies and water. Finally they reached Le Havre, France, on August 8. The crossing had taken 62 days, a record still unbeaten in spite of more recent attempts. Following exhibitions of the skiff in Europe they returned on a steamer, but 250 miles outside New York the ship ran out of coal. Once again the "Fox" was put on the water and Samuelson and Harbo rowed her back to New York to get assistance for the helpless vessel.

By Land, Sea and Air

BY LAND, SEA AND AIR

THE IRON HORSE came to Norway in the middle of the nineteenth century. In March 1851 the Parliament voted to construct a railroad from Christiania (Oslo) to the village of Eidsvoll, a distance of 42.5 miles. Robert Stephenson, the son of the famous English inventor George Stephenson, was invited to supervise the Norwegian project. He brought with him 50 English workers, who along with 1,500 Norwegians, managed to finish the task in 1854 in spite of many difficulties, human as well as mechanical. The opening trip to Eidsvoll, where 40 years earlier the Constitution had been adopted, was in itself a tremendous event for the Norwegian community. A whole new era came into being. Along with the huffing and puffing steam engine, which scared some, delighted many and impressed everyone, came new vistas and new promises for the saga-old country, which had been reborn four decades earlier at Eidsvoll. The awakening industries, now aspiring for foreign markets, were presented with a new transport instrument. The impact of the Norwegian railroad system on the development of the country is not easily measured. Facts and figures from the official statistics may render an extremely qualified version, yet the most fascinating story has been told by the trains themselves, from the first crude accommodations for the passengers to the sleek, streamlined coaches which daily penetrate the interior, linking rural areas to the cities and to each other, factories to shipping ports and country to country. Every express train speeding through the night and every freight train rambling from depot to depot is a reminder of the vital importance the railroad embodies and displays. The trains of Norway do not carry bold or historical names as do their American counterparts. It is the Bergensbanen, the Numedalsbanen, the Solørbanen, and the Urskog-Hølandsbanen, rather than the "Twentieth Century," the "Trailblazer," the "Hiawatha," the "Red Arrow," the "North Star," or the "Twilight Steeler." The Norwegian imagination has not gone further than "Dovregubben" (Mountain King), which hauls the trains between Oslo and Trondheim.

The magnificent railroad called Bergensbanen, linking the cities of Oslo and Bergen, was completed in 1909 and is regarded as one of the major achievements in railroad history. By offering to travelers a cross section of Norwegian scenery—smiling valleys, rolling fields, snow, ice and rock, and then the deep fjords—this line added a whole new dimension to the general trade and commerce picture of the nation. The Bergensbanen was wrested from a reluctant nature in a never-ending struggle for supremacy, and it is admired by experts and laymen alike, a highlight among the tourist attractions. The singing steels of the railroad are vibrating in the life of the country. Bergensbanen is about 300 miles long, has 270 tunnels and its highest point is at Taugevatn, 4,620 feet above sea level.

The railroads of Norway are operated by the state (Norges Stats Baner) and today comprise 2,790 miles of track. About 60 percent are electrically operated.

The captivating and fascinating story of Norwegian shipping is as old as the dragon-headed prows of the

Viking ships, yet as new as the newest cargo liner or
tanker launched last week. It is as the drama of a storm-
tossed vessel, going down with men who dedicated their
lives and work to the Seven Seas, and the pride felt by
Norwegians all over the globe, when "their" ships are
moored along piers among vessels of other great maritime nations.

A saga like this, spanning centuries and oceans, has
not only affected the Norwegians in a profound way econ-
omically, but has also stirred their imagination, creating
a feeling of personal involvement as if every Norwegian
were a shareholder in this great undertaking of the "float-
ing empire" that is Norwegian shipping. In a way they all
are. They feel thoroughly integrated with, and part of, the
expansion and general progress of the sprawling, dynamic
enterprise which constitutes the merchant marine. They
feel personally involved in the tremendous task of carry-
ing on a tradition as old as Norway herself. The Norwegian commercial fleet of today ties the sea glories of the
past to the promise for the future. The past was, at least
at the turn of the last century, a rather strenuous transi-
tory period. Norway in the 1870's had the third largest
merchant fleet in the world, exceeded only by Great Britain and the United States. By the beginning of the twentieth century her tonnage of sailing ships was twice as
large as that with steam power. In the historically crucial
year of 1905 the position was reversed. Slowly but steadily a new shipping era was developing.

It was rather natural that very early the emigrated Norwegians became vitally interested in a Norwegian national
shipping line to provide a direct connection with the Old
Country. Most of them had traveled on a "foreign line."
As early as 1871 an organized attempt to establish a Norwegian service had been made, but without success. Later,

leading shipping men in Norway, in search of capital, came to America to get in touch with prominent Norwegian-Americans. At one point the sale of stock in America exceeded that in Norway. It seems the Norwegians in America were inclined to look at the undertaking not simply as a business venture, but also as a meritorious national cause. The Norwegian America Line was founded in Norway on August 27, 1910. The first liner, S/S Kristianiafjord, was delivered May 22, 1913, and left Norway on her maiden voyage on June 7, arriving in New York ten days later.

During the early part of World War II the exiled but free Norwegian government contributed the entire national fleet to the Allied cause. The losses from this wartime period include more than 50 percent of the tonnage and some 3,000 Norwegian sailors. The shipowners virtually had to start the post-war period from scratch. Today the fleet sailing under the Norwegian flag is the youngest in age (averaging less than three years per ton). The fleet is active on almost all trade routes and the leader in shipboard automation, with such innovations as unmanned engine rooms. Significantly, the merchant marine has developed without direct government subsidies or special financial assistance. Altogether there are some 350 separate shipping companies throughout Norway. Of 3,000 ocean ships in foreign trade operations, half are oil tankers, with many vessels in excess of 200,000 tons. Norwegian shipowners are also pushing construction and operation of highly specialized carriers such as for liquified gas, newsprint and automobiles. In addition a number of new large luxury ships have been built to make Norway a leader in the cruise business.

While Norway has only 0.1 percent of the world population, the nation now has the fourth largest active mari-

time fleet in the world, close to 20 million gross tons. Over
the last two decades radical changes have taken place in
the manning of this fleet. Out of a total of 60,000 men
and women employed on board, about 12,700 are non-
nationals of Norway. They represent 35 different nations,
mostly from Continental Europe but almost as many from
Asiatic countries, North and South America, Africa and
Australia. Most Europeans are Spanish or Yugoslavian.
Of a total of close to 5,000 women on board the ships,
comparatively few are from Norway. All ship masters and
most other officers are Norwegian.

The welfare of the seamen in the Norwegian fleet in
foreign ports is the concern of the privately operated Norwegian Seamen's Mission, founded in 1863 and headquartered in Bergen, Norway, and of the State Welfare
Council for the Merchant Fleet, financed through contributions from seamen and shipowners.

One of the strongest links between the merchant fleet of
Norway and Norwegians ashore has been forged by The
Society of Ship Adoption, which today includes more than
one thousand schools all over the country.

The Society was formed in 1939. After World War II
it was reactivated and has since increased its scope of activities considerably. Other countries, among them the
United States, have followed suit.

Originally, the whole ship adoption idea was simply
based on the exchange of letters between school children
and the officials and crews manning the vessels. Letters
sent and received were posted on the bulletin boards in the
schools and on board the ships. In all their simplicity
these letters written by children carried a message of substantial strength to those seamen. Many of the oldtimers
had not seen their families and home towns for several
years and these letters often had a great impact. They

reported to the seamen in their native language the ordinary day-to-day happenings in their districts. Trivia suddenly assumed great significance when measured by the vast distance between ship and school.

As this shore-sea contact has grown, the "getting-to-know-you" stage has developed into new phases and aspects. Letters turned into regular newspapers, with photos pasted on the stencilled pages, news items and articles, interviews and stories told by the children. Mail boxes are hung in the school corridors and emptied at regular intervals. Clippings from local newspapers and other publications are added to the sizable package finally dispatched to the adopted vessel. The use of tape recorders has added another promising development. Taped programs from a number of traditional school functions, such as Christmas parties, 17th of May celebrations, graduation ceremonies with speeches, songs and music, are highly welcomed by the seamen half a world away from home.

They, in turn, send gifts to "their schools" such as tropical fruits, fossil plant collections, snakes and other animals, ship models, strange-looking shells, souvenirs of all kinds, coins, stamps, pictures and newspapers, periodicals, spears, bows and arrows. One day a school class received a large parcel from Sidney, Australia. The children found an honest-to-goodness boomerang and the whole class promptly went outside to try it. The only sad part was that it never returned. After a three hour search it was finally retrieved from high up in a pine tree. Perhaps they do not have that kind of tree in the land down under.

The world map hanging in the class room becomes a focal point each time a letter or parcel arrives. Ship positions are pinpointed and the route is traced with pencil lines. Where is she right now? What kind of cargo does she carry? Information provided in the letters serves as essay material and prizes are sent by the ship for essay contests: "We are going to Venezuela to take in oil. We are headed for Casablanca with general cargo. We are bound for Baltimore with cars. We have left Hong Kong and are going through the Panama Canal, bound for Italy. Our next mailing address will be Rio de Janeiro. What do you know about these countries and cities? We have been there, but frankly we don't know too much about the history and people. Can you help us?" The boys and girls are eager to assist them with their own learning from the books in the school library. Sometimes they rearrange the class room furniture and give the pieces new names, lifted from the nautical terminology. The room is no longer a room. It is a ship with bridge, engine room, look-out, cabins and galleys. They man their "vessel," each with his own specific job. They live and relive the letters and pictures received.

Then a cherished dream comes true. The Captain cables that his ship will call at a nearby Norwegian port in a few weeks, and the whole class is invited to visit the adopted vessel. Dressed in their Sunday-best, the eager children arrive on a bus furnished by the shipping company. The Captain and his officers welcome them as true guests of honor. The youngsters swarm all over the ship from stem to stern. They meet all their pen pals who show them around, explaining the ship and describing wonderful places beyond the horizon. Some of the children have studied the specifications of the vessel so well that they virtually know their way around without any help at all. In their shining eyes is reflected a yearning for the life at sea. In fact, the ship adoption program in Norway has contributed considerably to the recruitment for the fleet. Before leaving port, the Captain and some of his staff and crew may find time to visit the school, give speeches, and show films and photos. They also will discuss possible improvements in the program with the principal and teachers.

Weeks pass. Then another letter arrives and the Captain reports that the students from a little school in Takoradi, the Gold Coast, have visited his ship and admired a picture from the part of Norway where the ship's school is located. He tells about the school and the children that "own" his ship and suggests that they send a greeting. Their letter reads:

"It is a great pleasure to send you a collection of some of our work. Our friend the Captain has told us about you and how you work in your school high up in the mountains. We expect that you have to wear sweaters and furs to keep warm while we try to keep cool by wearing cotton clothes. Our school is held on the porch of a long, low, wooden building. We have sixteen students, six of them are in the nursery. Our ages range from five to fourteen. Serious working in the heat is difficult, but we do our best. Will you write us and tell about your school. We would like to start a pen-friendship. May we wish you, your parents and teachers happiness . . ." And so a new dimension is added to the adoption program. As one ship captain observed, "This contact between schools of many nations is more valuable than all the peace conferences put together."

Aviation came to Norway in 1912 when the Government secured a plane for military purposes. The same year the first six Norwegian aviation licenses were issued, and the following year the first Norway-built aircraft was ready for operation.

As early as 1870, however, the first man-made flying object had appeared in the Norwegian skies. Paris was surrounded by German armies, isolated from the rest of the country. The only way to communicate with the outside world was by air, and the French used a number of balloons, each containing 70,000 cubic feet of gas with 4x4x3 foot wicker baskets seating four persons.

One third of the crews were sailors as it was felt that sea navigation was not too different from air navigation. On November 24, 1870, in the face of a raging storm, the balloon *La Ville d'Orleans* left Paris, piloted by Paul-Valery Rolier, 26 year old civil engineer. Together with a guerilla fighter, Leon Bezier, age 30, he had volunteered for this trip. The following morning the balloonists were over the North Sea drifting northwest at a speed of approximately 50 m.p.h. After 15 hours of flight they finally landed in the mountainous district of Telemark in Norway. The balloon, however, continued to travel and was spotted by a number of people who of course had rather mixed reactions to this first UFO in the history of Norway. When it finally came down, a young boy removed six live pigeons, some books and fresh food from the basket. Meanwhile, the aviators themselves found their way to an empty mountain cottage and later met two farmers who brought them down to the village and to their pastor, who in turn sent for a French-speaking engineer. The daring Frenchmen eventually were brought to Kristiania (Oslo) where they were accorded a hero's reception and where the balloon basket, anchor and other items from the bizarre flight may still be seen. In Telemark a commemorative stone has been placed at the landing spot. On the first anniversary of the flight Paul-Valery Rolier revisited Norway for a reunion with the Telemark farmers who found them.

Another highlight of early Norwegian aviation history occurred in the fall of 1914 when Tryggve Gran, a young pilot, became the first to cross the North Sea by plane. He flew from Scotland to the district of Jären in southwestern Norway. This feat, however, was completely overshadowed by the outbreak of World War I. After the war the first

Norwegian airline came into being, *Det Norske Luftfartssel-skap*, (DNL) and the Bergen-Stavanger route opened in 1920. Other companies were formed in the 1930's and today Norway has an excellent domestic air traffic network.

A major development concerning the Scandinavian air interests took place in 1946 when the Scandinavian Airlines System was created by Denmark, Sweden and Norway. Their interests are divided in sevenths, with 2/7 for Norway. Today SAS employs about 13,000 persons, of which approximately 16 percent are flying personnel. More than 60 SAS planes serve 85 cities in 42 countries.

The most important airports in Norway are found at Oslo (Fornebu), Stavanger (Sola), Bergen (Flesland), Trondheim (Värnes), Kristiansand (Kjevik), Bodø, Bardufoss and Høybuktmoen in North Norway.

A Fjord in Your Future

A FJORD IN YOUR FUTURE

"THERE'S A FJORD IN Your Future!" . . .

So it is claimed in colorful ads, articles, posters, folders, and photos by the organizations which work for ever-increasing travel to Norway—the Land of the Midnight Sun.

Statistics seem to confirm predictions. In 1973 close to 900,000 non-Nordic tourists were registered in Norway, and found their way to the Norwegian fjords, mountains, glaciers, forests, valleys, and Vigeland sculptures. In addition, about 200,000 Swedes, Danes, and Finns "dropped in" for a one-day visit. Mr. Per Prag, Director of the Norwegian National Travel Office in New York, pondered these various figures and stated, "One can only be happy for the fact that they didn't all arrive at the same time!"

Of the total number of tourists more than 190,000 came from the United States. The other non-Scandinavian visitors came mainly from Germany, Great Britain, France, the Netherlands, and Italy.

The total income from the travel trade in 1973 was estimated at close to $300,000,000.

The main source of this sizeable contribution to the Norwegian coffers is of course the spectacular mountain and fjord scenery, sparkling lakes and glaciers and mountains so numerous that many Norwegians insist they had to be put on top of each other in order to make room for all of them. All these scenic attractions, combined with friendly hospitality, an abundance of excellent food and a variety of travel pleasures at moderate prices must be the reason for this increasing invasion which knows no season.

No visas are needed by U.S. citizens visiting Norway. A valid passport is the only document required and border formalities are reduced to a minimum. For re-entry into the United States, travelers need a smallpox vaccination certificate less than three years old. The Norwegian customs inspections are smooth and courteous. Personal effects will never cause difficulty. U.S. travelers (over age 17) may bring in, free of duty, up to 400 cigarettes or 50 cigars, and one quart of liquor and wine. Up to $500 worth of souvenirs may also be brought in duty-free but must be taken out of Norway again upon departure. Samples and goods for exhibits are granted temporary duty-free admission. Gifts mailed from the United States to persons in Norway may be allowed duty-free entry provided the value is less than about $15.

There are no restrictions on importing U.S. currency but it is advisable for visitors to declare their dollars on arrival to avoid difficulty in taking out unspent money. Only limited amounts of Norwegian currency may be brought in or out; the import limit is 1,000 Kroner and export limit 350 Kroner. Travelers' checks can be cashed everywhere in Norway. Norwegians going abroad are allowed to buy foreign currency up to about $700 plus $50 in Norwegian currency. American and Canadian citizens who own money in Norway may spend it during personal visits. If they should wish to convert their funds into dollars for transfer, applications must be forwarded through their bank in Norway.

Norway's climate is much milder than one might expect this far north. It is definitely "more solar than polar" thanks to the gentle caresses of the Gulf Stream.

From early May until late August the sun brightens the nights and lengthens the days, giving the traveler added hours for sightseeing. An average June day in Oslo has over nineteen hours of sunlight. Above the Arctic Circle the sun never sets at all during the summer and the whole disk of the sun is visible at night, glowing in colors that become more fabulous as midnight approaches.

As for clothes, medium-weight garments are recommended as a basis for the tourist's wardrobe. Include a raincoat, a topcoat for spring and fall, and an overcoat or fur coat for late fall and winter. Formal clothes are not needed in summer. The traveler will have more use for sports clothes, the same as one would pick for vacations in the United States, but with extra emphasis on tweeds and woolens. Good, heavy walking shoes are a must for comfort.

Visitors with electric shavers, irons and similar travel appliances are advised to bring only those appliances which are equipped with adapters for use of electric current which varies in voltage from 110 to 220, A.C. and D.C., and in cycles from 50 to 60. Prongs for outlets also differ from those in the United States.

Picturesque Norway is a camper's paradise. As a matter of fact there are few, if any, countries in Western Europe where camping prospects are brighter. Apart from the areas around the towns, it is possible to pitch a tent almost anywhere in ideal surroundings. However, the majority of motorists and campers stick to the sites operated by the automobile associations, municipalities and private owners, where parking and other arrangements are better.

Over two hundred rivers provide salmon and sea trout.

The season extends from June until September, and some of the best salmon fishing in the world can be had in these rivers. Besides rivers, Norway is honeycombed with innumerable lakes — nearly 250,000 — scattered all over the country. There are trout in practically every lake and river, even high up in the mountain ranges. Generally speaking trout fishing is good from the end of May until mid-September.

In a few hours' walk from any road or railway a hiker can reach the beautiful mountain districts off the beaten track. Tourist lodges, offering good beds and substantial meals, are found at intervals corresponding to a day's walk. This network of *turisthytter* has made hiking extremely popular. The routes between the lodges are clearly marked so even inexperienced walkers can safely set out into the mountains. Although most peaks have been climbed, there is still scope for further exploring of new routes. All popular climbs are well marked.

If American parents should wish to see a bit more of Europe than Norway, and minus their children, they may happily park them there. Healthy, open-air life is the hallmark of supervised children's camps which are located on the fjords and in the mountain ranges. Teenagers, too, will enjoy staying at the modern youth hostels, the most reasonable in Europe.

As for pets, it is not easy to bring them to Norway. It requires an import permit which generally is issued only under exceptional circumstances. One must be able to verify that his pet is free from infectious diseases, and in the case of dogs that the district of origin has been rabies-free for the last twelve months. Such a certificate needs the endorsement of the nearest Norwegian Consulate. The import permit, issued by the Norwegian Department of Agriculture in advance, must be produced upon arrival.

All pets will be put in quarantine in Norway for a period of seven months. There is no dispensation from the rule. The one and only such quarantine is in Oslo. When leaving Norway one is free to take his pet without any formalities.

Probably the best and most inexpensive shopping spree in the whole of Europe can be had in Norway. Among best buys are silver articles with inlaid enamel work, handicraft of many shapes and patterns, pewter of Viking Age design, crystal, handknit sweaters, fur coats and stoles, ceramics, handwoven textiles, furniture, fishing rods and cutlery. Century-old antiques are in abundance at shops where contemporary art works are also available. Souvenir articles such as wood carvings, whale tooth carvings, dolls in national costumes, sealskin boots, elk skin items, handwrought iron, wooden trays and salad sets of teak, not to mention ski equipment, are also indeed eye-appealing, beautiful and useful.

Shopping hours are generally from 8:30 a.m. to 5 p.m. on weekdays and to 4 p.m. on Saturdays. Local souvenir shops are usually kept open Sundays.

Norwegian clothing sizes are different from those in the United States. The traveler may wish to refer to Appendix E in this book for a comparison chart.

Norway is easy to reach from any point in the United States via numerous air and sea connections with convenient Norwegian gateways. In addition, Norway has an extensive modern transportation network of ships, planes, trains and buses offering the traveler highly diversified itineraries. Fine hotels and restaurants are found everywhere throughout the country.

Adding to the fun of visiting the land of one's ancestors is the hobby of digging for the ancestors themselves. It appeals to the sense of belonging to have a family tree with names and dates on almost every branch. Of course there is also some risk — like coming across an ancestor who was not exactly the pride of his medieval community. Perhaps he was convicted and hanged for horse stealing by his less understanding neighbors. On the other hand there might have been some who distinguished themselves and became pillars of their local society.

If you have made up your mind to do some research on your own to find out about your ancestry or simply to track down some of your relatives who may still be living in Norway, there are quite a number of official and private agencies and persons prepared to assist you.

First of all you must decide exactly what you want to find out. You must restrict your search and perhaps try to trace back one line of the family first and then take the others in turn. Or you can concentrate on a particular branch of the family which has lived, generation after generation, in the same place.

You must also realize that it is sometimes difficult to trace the lineage of your ancestors very far back. This may be due to a number of different reasons. The information you start with may be so vague that it is impossible to know where to begin the search. Your ancestors may have moved about so much that it is hopeless to keep track of them. Important sources of information may have been destroyed. Even in the most favorable circumstances it is often difficult to trace a family farther back than to the second half of the 17th century, for the simple reason that few consecutive records were kept before this time.

It matters a great deal what your ancestors were — whether they were farmers working on the same farm for generations, whether they were workers or servants, public officials or merchants, seamen or fishermen. According to their occupation some families are easier to trace than others. In general, do not be surprised if quite a considerable expenditure of time and money yields only a modest amount of information.

Before you visit or write to Norway, assemble all the information you can obtain in the United States. Such information may be from relatives and friends, letters, certificates, notations in old Bibles or even on photos. Information may also be obtained from official institutions, archives and libraries, from records relating to immigration, employment, naturalization, military service, marriage and death. Even inscriptions on tombstones can be useful.

In the United States you may contact Sons of Norway International Headquarters, 1455 West Lake Street, Minneapolis, Minnesota 55408 or the Norwegian-American Historical Association, St. Olaf College, Northfield, Minnesota. Biographies and histories may also be consulted at major libraries such as the Library of Congress, Washington, D. C. and a number of libraries of various universities and colleges throughout the country. The Genealogical Society of the Church of Jesus Christ of Latter Day Saints, Salt Lake City, Utah, has film copies of all the principal genealogical records in Norway and other European countries.

There are also other things you should do before you approach the primary sources in Norway. You should write to your relatives in Norway, if you have their address. They can often give you valuable information and will probably know whether any history of your family has been written. Perhaps your family, or at any rate a branch of it, has already been charted. You can also write to one of the principal libraries in Norway: *Universitetsbiblioteket,* (The University Library), Oslo; *Universitetsbiblioteket,* Bergen; *Videnskapsselskapets Bibliotek* (Library of the Scientific Society), Trondheim; *Deichmanske Bibliotek,* Oslo.

The *bygdebøker* (rural chronicles) are the best source

of information about typical farming families.

Norsk Slektshistorisk Forening (Norwegian Genealogical Society), *Øvre Slottsgate* 17, Oslo, will also be able to provide information.

Surnames should be given special attention. Emigrants often stopped using the name of the family farm in Norway as their surname and adopted their father's Christian name instead with the suffix -sen (-son). Emigrants were not very particular about which surname they adopted. It happened that Ole Halvorsen and his son Halvor Olsen adopted the same surname, Halvorsen or Olsen. In the United States, for instance, names such as Nelson, Johnson and Anderson were already widely known and much easier to pronounce than most Norwegian farm names. Even in the few cases where the farm name was retained as a surname, it was often so much changed and modified under the influence of the new language that it became unrecognizable. The best account of farm names in Norway is found in the large work called *Norske Gaardsnavne*.

When you have assembled all the information you can secure in your own country, from relatives in Norway, and from written sources, the time has come to consult the primary sources. These include the many kinds of records which have been kept through the centuries, chiefly by official institutions, and they are listed in Appendix F.

SAFE IN THE ARMS OF MOTHER NORWAY

HAVING ACHIEVED the age of one hundred, an Oslo old-timer once was asked if he had any advice on how to reach such a respectable milestone. The centenarian calmly replied, "Just continue to breathe, young man!" Aside from this rather logical response, and as previously mentioned in this book, the life expectancy for the average Norwegian is very high, perhaps higher than in any other nation. Major reasons for this remarkable ability to hang on at an age when most others have departed for the proverbial pastures, might be listed as: (1) stubbornness as a national trait; (2) a deep-rooted love for fellow Norwegians; (3) the possibility of witnessing another Norwegian victory over Sweden in a soccer match; (4) to find out what Thor Heyerdahl will be up to next; (5) to have another go at lutefisk and other national goodies; and (6) continued enjoyment of the blessings of a multitude of social legislative provisions.

At this point it might be in order to note that, according to the American researcher Dr. Herbert Hendin who is associated with Columbia University Psychoanalytic Clinic, Norwegians are less prone to suicide than the Danes and the Swedes. In his work *Suicide and Scandinavia,* Dr. Hendin notes that the suicide rates in the two other countries are three times as high as in Norway. He does not accept the theory that the heavy emigration to America is a main factor of the low Norwegian suicide rate. It has always been low, regardless of the great fluctuations of the emigration waves, he states, adding that more plausible reasons include the fact that Norwegian youngsters learn at an early age to become independent and stand on their own feet. Comparing the Norwegians with the Swedes, Dr. Hendin observes that the Norwegians do not press so hard for success and high goals as the Swedes who thereby subject themselves to more pressure.

If not exactly explosive, Norway's development in social welfare fields encompassing the entire population has indeed been rapid and thorough. While at an early stage of the Norwegian community, problems arising from illness, old age and an assortment of other contingencies were exclusively dealt with by the family itself. The Church gradually handled special emergencies which the family was unable to take care of. Only in the mid-1800s were the first communally organized steps taken to bring about active participation in social work. The Parliament, in 1845, enacted a proposal concerning parish relief. It stated that anyone in material need was entitled to public support. The first health acts were also adopted at the same time. The industrial revolution, paired with an elevated educational standard, necessitated acts concerning factory inspection and occupational injuries. In 1919 another law limited the working day to eight hours. During the 1920s and early 1930s no essential progress was made in sociopolitical fields. Then, in rapid succession, came acts protecting workers, fishermen, blind, crippled, and handicapped persons. During the immediate post-World War II years, the solid foundation was laid for a welfare state along lines comparable to those in other Norse nations, with a complete social security system for all as the ultimate goal.

Acts providing assistance to disabled, widows, and

mothers came into being. So did a state housing loan system, and acts dealing with a national pension plan, social care and improved financial circumstances for elderly persons. Of prime importance during recent years has been the rehabilitation of handicapped persons, the basic principle being help to self-help.

All problems relating to child welfare receive high priority in Norway. Each municipality must appoint a child welfare council to supervise the conditions under which children and young people live. Numerous children's homes, supervised by the council, are either publicly or privately managed, most of them receiving public financial support. The School Medical and Dental Services are also well organized. In Oslo, the internationally known "Oslo Breakfast" continues to attract the attention of experts from other countries. The breakfasts are served forty-five finutes before school starts. The breakfast takes thirty minutes, followed by a fifteen minute break in open air.

Children's insurance was introduced by law in 1946, ensuring a fixed payment for anyone who supports more than one child. Payments for each child continue up to the age of sixteen. The Mother's Insurance System, a great social reform, safeguards finances in families where the father is missing. Its aim is to provide financial aid to these families, so that the mother need not wear herself out doing paid work and thereby possibly neglecting her children. In homes where there are small children and the mother is prevented from looking after them, due to illness or some similar problem, a "deputy housewife" or Home Help may be called in as a substitute. Time of service in each instance is limited to three weeks, and the homes pay a small fee to the municipality for this service, fixed on a sliding scale, according to the income of the family. Prior to World War II, juvenile delinquency accounted for some

29 percent of all crimes committed. The figure has since been climbing, with car thefts being the major problem. Children under the age of fourteen cannot be brought before a criminal court, while young offenders between fourteen and eighteen years are usually referred to the child welfare committees. In cases where the youth involved is between the ages of eighteen and twenty-three, the offender may be placed in a vocational training school instead of being sent to prison.

A more recent development is the fact the days of every Norwegian citizen are "numbered." Each individual residing in Norway receives an eleven-digit birth number for his very own. Even though one need not introduce the person at social functions as "Mr. 1234" or "Mrs. 5678", the number will follow the individual from the cradle to the grave.

The new system is not at all similar to the Social Security numbers of Americans. The purpose is primarily to facilitate the control of amounts received and paid out between state institutions and the citizen, and to insure that the person can be found more quickly in the public registers. Particularly in the internal revenue files, it can be assumed! Now then, how is the birth number arrived at? For an example, look at the number 30 10 43 419 81:

30 signifies that the owner was born on the thirtieth day of the month;

10 that the birth took place in the tenth month of the year;

43 means the year of birth was 1943;

419 are three individual digits. If the first is less than 5, the owner was born in the 1900s. If the digit is 5, 6, or 7, the birth took place in the 1800s. If the third individual digit is 1, 3, 5, 7 or 9, the

person is male. If the digit is 0, 2, 4, 6 or 8, the person is female.

81 are two control digits.

The most recent and by far the most comprehensive national social security system was introduced in 1967, replacing a series of existing regulations. The basic philosophy involved was that elderly persons should have a living standard which resembled the one obtained during the years of active employment. At pension age, which is seventy, persons receive a basic as well as a supplementary pension. In addition, certain extra benefits are available. In Oslo, the capital city, free medical treatment and free medicine are provided in cases where such expenses are not covered by statute or by health insurance, and free baths are available at the municipal baths. Elderly people pay reduced rates when traveling by public transportation, and they are invited to attend shows, concerts, and other events without cost.

While the state and local authorities are constantly engaged in preparing, proposing and implementing short and long term socio-political programs, it should be stressed that a close working relationship exists between private voluntary organizations and the government. Some of the major voluntary organizations and societies are the Norwegian Red Cross (Norges Røde Kors), Norwegian People's Relief (Norsk Folkehjelp), Norwegian Women's Health Organization (Norske Kvinners Sanitetsforening), National Organization for the Promotion of Public Health (Nasjonalforeiningen for Folkehelsen); National Organization Against Cancer (Landsforeningen mot Kreft), and the National Association against Tuberculosis (Nasjonalforeningen mot Tuberkulose). They all have rendered a remarkable, dedicated service for decades. The last one mentioned has a branch of such unique character that it merits special comment.

Almost fifty years ago Mr. Ditlef Frantzen, the local postmaster in the idyllic village of Nesbyen, Hallingdal, in central Norway, conceived the idea of collecting and marketing cancelled stamps for the purpose of raising funds to help finance the work by the Association for children threatened by tuberculosis. Some of the funds are also used for handicapped children. Named TUBFRIM, this initially modest project today employs more than forty persons and annually processes millions of stamps pouring in from all parts of the world. More than three-hundred thousand dollars in funds have been netted and distributed as a result of this global assistance.

The major contribution of stamps has come from the United States, with Sons of Norway taking the lead supported by the Girl Scouts, veterans organizations, Masonic groups, church congregations, women's clubs, Merchant Marines, and tens of thousands of individuals all over America. TUBFRIM sells the stamps to collectors throughout the world. All kinds of postage stamps are accepted, but the large commemorative stamps issued are particularly valuable.

Norway's social assistance structure is indeed a protective umbrella covering the entire country.

APPENDIX A
WHO'S WHO OF NORWEGIANS
AND AMERICANS BORN IN NORWAY

A

ABEL, Niels Henrik (1800-1829). Regarded as one of the world's greatest mathematicians of the 19th century.

AMUNDSEN, Roald Engebregt Graving (1872-1928). Polar explorer. First to find the Northwest Passage (1906); first at the South Pole (1911); first across the North Pole with dirigible airship NORGE (1926).

ASBJØRNSEN, Peter Christen (1812-1885). Co-collector with Jørgen Moe of folk and fairy tales.

B

BALCHEN, Bernt (1899-   ). American aviator and explorer. Flew the Atlantic in 1927; to the South Pole in 1929. First to become an American citizen by Congressional Act since Lafayette.

BENNETT, Thomas B. (1814-1898). Travel business pioneer.

BJELLAND, Christian (1858-1927). Founder of the canning industry in Stavanger, "Canning Capital of the World."

BJERKNES, Jacob Aall Bonnevie (1897-   ). Professor of Meteorology, University of California. Awarded the 1966 Congressional National Medal of Science.

BJØRNSON, Bjørnstjerne (1832-1910). Wrote the National Anthem (*"Ja, vi elsker dette landet"*).

BULL, Ole Bornemann (1810-1880). Violinist, composer, and founder of the colony Oleana in Pennsylvania.

C

CHRISTENSEN, Lars (1884-1965). Shipowner specializing in whaling and sponsor of scientific Antartic expeditions.

C

COLLETT, Jacobine Camilla (1813-1895). Writer and pioneer of women's rights movement. Sister of poet Henrik Wergeland.

D

DASS, Petter (1647-1707). Theologian and writer.

DUUN, Olav Julius (1876-1939). Novelist.

E

EGEDE, Hans Poulsen (1686-1758). First Norwegian missionary to Greenland.

EYDE, Samuel (1866-1940). Industrialist and founder of large NORSK HYDRO concern.

F

FALKBERGET, Johan Petter (1879-1967). Novelist.

FALSEN, Christian Magnus (1782-1830). Author of the Constitution adopted at Eidsvoll, May 17, 1814.

FLAGSTAD, Kirsten Målfrid (1895-1962). Opera and concert singer. Head of the Norwegian Opera in Oslo established after World War II.

FOYN, Svend (1809-1894). Whaling and sealing pioneer through his invention of the grenade harpoon gun.

FRISCH, Ragnar (1895-   ). Professor of economics at the University of Oslo. First recipient of Nobel prize for economics in 1969.

FURUSETH, Andrew (1854-1938). Organizer of American seamen. Called the "Abraham Lincoln of the Seas."

G

GARBORG, Arne (1851-1924). Novelist and poet.

GIAEVER, Ivar (1930-   ). Nobel prize winner in physics, 1973.

GRIEG, Edvard Hagerup (1843-1907). Composer.

H

HAMBRO, Carl Joachim (1885-1964). Statesman and writer.

HAMSUN, Knut (1859-1952). Novelist and poet.

HASSEL, Odd (1897-   ). Professor in Physical Chemistry at the University of Oslo. 1969 Nobel prize for chemistry.

HAUGE, Hans Nielsen (1771-1824). Evangelist and starter of the Haugianism movement.

HENIE, Sonja (1912-1969). Olympic and World figure skating champion, movie star and pioneer of ice shows.

HEYERDAHL, Thor (1914-   ). Ethnologist and zoologist achieving world fame through his Kon-Tiki raft expedition in 1947, and "Ra II" Atlantic crossing in 1970.

HOLBERG, Ludvig (1684-1754). Norwegian-Danish writer and scientist.

I

IBSEN, Henrik Johan (1828-1906). Playwright and poet.

INGSTAD, Helge Marcus (1899-   ). Explorer, scientist and writer. Located Viking settlements in North America.

J

JAHRE, Anders August (1891-   ). Shipowner and philanthropist.

K

KIELLAND, Alexander Lange (1849-1906). Writer.

KITTELSEN, Theodor Severin (1857-1914). Painter, writer and illustrator of folk and fairy tales.

KNUDSEN, Aanon Gunerius (Gunnar) (1848-1928). Prime Minister 1908-10, 1913-20.

KROHG, Christian (1852-1925). Painter. Particularly known in America for his work "Leiv Eiriksson Discovers America."

KROHG, Per (1889-1965). Painter. Among his works is the mural in the U. N. Security Council Room, New York.

L

LANDSTAD, Magnus Brostrup (1802-1880). Theologian and hymn writer.

LIE, Jonas Lauritz Idemil (1833-1908). Novelist and poet.

LIE, Trygve Halvdan (1896-1968). Statesman. First Secretary General of the United Nations.

M

MATHISEN, Oscar (1888-1954). Norway's first speed skating "king" with numerous World, European and Norwegian championships and records.

MICHELSEN, Peter Christian Hersleb Kjerschow (1857-1925). Prime Minister during the 1905 dissolution of the Norway-Sweden Union.

MOE, Jørgen (1813-1882). Theologian and co-collector of folk and fairy tales with Peter C. Asbjørnsen.

MUNCH, Edvard (1863-1944). Painter. Most of his works are at the Edvard Munch Museum in Oslo.

N

NANSEN, Fridtjof (1861-1930). Scientist, explorer, writer, statesman and humanitarian. Instigator of the Nansen Passport for refugees.

NELSON, Knute (1843-1923). U.S. Senator from Minnesota.

NORDRAAK, Richard (1842-1866). Composer of the music for the National Anthem *"Ja, vi elsker dette landet."*

NYGAARDSVOLD, Johan (1879-1952). Prime Minister 1935-1945, including World War II when the government resided in London.

O

ONSAGER, Lars (1903-   ). Professor at Yale University. Nobel Prize Winner in Chemistry 1968, and recipient of the Congressional National Medal of Science.

R

RIISER-LARSEN, Hjalmar (1890-1965). Aviator and explorer. Headed the Norwegian Air Force during World War II. "One World" President, 1951-57.

ROLVAAG, Ole (1876-1931). Author and professor at St. Olaf College, Northfield, Minnesota.

S

SINGSTAD, Ole (1882-1969). Civil engineer and world's leading authority on tunnel construction. Designer of Holland, Queens Midtown and Battery Tunnels, New York and Baltimore Harbor Tunnel, Baltimore, Maryland.

SOYLAND, Carl (1894-   ). Editor emeritus of Norwegian language paper *Nordisk Tidende,* Brooklyn, New York. Author and poet.

SINDING, Christian August (1856-1941). Composer.

SIVLE, Per (Peder) (1857-1904). Novelist and poet.

SVERDRUP, Leif (1898-   ). Civil engineer and officer. Constructed more than 200 airfields in the Pacific during World War II.

SÄVERUD, Harald (1897-   ). Composer.

T

THRANE, Marcus Møller (1817-1890). Labor organizer, editor and author.

TORDENSKJOLD, Peter Wessel (1691-1720). Naval hero.

U

UNDSET, Sigrid (1882-1949). Author. Awarded the Nobel Prize for Literature in 1928.

V

VIGELAND, Adolf Gustav (1869-1943). Sculptor.

VINJE, Aasmund Olavsson (1818-1870). Writer, poet and editor.

W

WELHAVEN, Johan Sebastian Cammermeyer (1807-1873). Poet.

WERENSKIOLD, Erik Theodor (1855-1938). Painter.

WERGELAND, Henrik Arnold (1808-1845). Poet and playwright. Initiated celebrations on Constitution Day, May 17.

WESSEL, Johan Herman (1742-1785). Satirical poet.

WILDENWEY, Herman Theodore (Portaas) (1886-1959). Poet.

Ø

ØVERLAND, Arnulf (1889-1968). Poet.

AA

AASEN, Ivar Andreas (1813-1896). Writer, poet and introducer of the New Norwegian language.

APPENDIX B

ORDSPRÅK	PROVERBS
Etter regn kommer solskinn.	Sunshine follows rain.
Det er ikke gull alt som glimrer.	All is not gold that glitters.
Liten tue kan velte stort lass.	Little strokes fell great oaks.
Hastverk er lastverk.	More haste, less speed. (Haste makes waste)
Like barn leker best.	Birds of a feather flock together.
Brent barn skyr ilden.	A burnt child avoids the fire. (Once bitten, twice shy)
Borte bra, men hjemme best.	East-West, home best.
Mange bekker små gjør en stor å.	Many small rivulets make a big brook. (Every little bit helps)
En skal ikke skue hunden på hårene.	Appearances are deceitful.
Kjärt barn har mange navn.	A pet child has many names.
Tomme tønner ramler mest.	Empty barrels are the noisiest.
I mørke er alle katter grå.	All cats are grey in the dark.

Når katten er borte danser musene på bordet.	When the cat is away the mice will play.
Som katten om den varme grøten.	Like a cat with too hot milk. (Beating around the bush)
En fugl i hånden er bedre enn ti på taket.	One bird in hand is worth two in the bush.
Spare på skillingen og la daleren rulle.	Save the pennies and let the dollar roll. (Penny wise and dollar foolish)
En må smi mens jernet er varmt.	Strike while the iron is hot.
En svale gjør ingen sommer.	One swallow does not make a summer.
Eplet faller ikke langt fra stammen.	The apple does not fall far from the tree.
Bite i det sure eple.	Take a bite of the sour apple.
Som man roper i skogen får en svar.	As you shout in the forest, so will the echo sound. (Ask a stupid question and you get a stupid answer)
Smuler er også brød.	Crumbs are also bread.
Hver fugl synger med sitt nebb.	Every bird sings with his own voice.

Den som det lille forsmår, det store ikke får.	One who disdains the little, does not get the big.
Nye koster feier best.	New brooms sweep clean.
Som man reder så ligger man.	As we make our bed, so we must lie.
Når enden er god er allting godt.	All's well that ends well.
Den som bor i glasshus bør ikke kaste stein.	Those who live in glass houses should not throw stones.
Den må krøkes i tide som god krok skal bli.	Training must begin early.
Den som ler sist ler best.	He who laughs last, laughs loudest.
En dåre kan spørre mer en ti vise kan svare.	One fool may ask more questions than ten wisemen can answer.
Nød lärer naken kvinne å spinne.	Necessity is the mother of invention.
Hunger er den beste kokk.	Hunger is the best sauce.
Når det regner på presten så drypper det på klokkeren.	If it rains on the preacher it drips on the sexton

*Renslighet er en dyd sa
kjerringa, hun vrengte
underkjolen hver julekveld.*

"Cleanliness is a virtue," said
the old woman turning her
shift inside out every
Christmas Eve.

*Stillest vann har dypest
grunn.*

Still water runs deep.

APPENDIX C
SOME EVERYDAY EXPRESSIONS AND WORDS

Yes	*Ja*
No	*Nei*
Please	*Vär så snill*
Excuse me	*Unnskyld*
Thanks	*Takk (Tusen Takk)*
You are welcome	*Ingen årsak*
What time is it?	*Hvor mye er klokken?*
Wait a moment	*Vent litt*
I beg your pardon	*Om forlatelse*
Good Morning	*God morgen*
Good Day	*God dag*
Good Night	*God natt*
Mother	*Mor*
Father	*Far*
Brother	*Bror*
Sister	*Søster*
Son	*Sønn*
Daughter	*Datter*
Uncle	*Onkel*
Aunt	*Tante*
How are you?	*Hvordan står det til?*
So long	*På gjensyn*
Phone	*Telefon*
Food	*Mat*
Bread	*Brød*
Butter	*Smør*
Happy Birthday	*Gratulerer med dagen*
Good Luck	*Lykke til*
Merry Christmas	*God Jul*
Happy New Year	*Godt Nyttår*
Bon Voyage	*God tur*
North	*Nord*
East	*Øst*
South	*Sør (syd)*
West	*Vest*
House	*Hus*
Street	*Gate*
Number	*Nummer*

One, two, three	*En, to, tre*
Four, five, six	*Fire, fem, seks*
Seven, eight, nine, ten	*Sju, åtte, ni, ti*
Right	*Høyre*
Left	*Venstre*
How much?	*Hvor mye?*
Car	*Bil*
Train	*Tog*
Boat	*Skip*
Plane	*Fly*
Keep Out	*Adgang Forbudt*
Movie	*Film*
Theater	*Teater*
Play	*Stykke*
No Smoking	*Røyking forbudt*
Closed	*Stengt*
Taxi	*Drosje*
Day	*Dag*
Week	*Uke*
Month	*Måned*
Year	*År*
Boy	*Gutt*
Girl	*Jente*
Breakfast	*Frokost*
Lunch	*Lunsj*
Dinner	*Middag*
Snack	*Smørbrød*
Money	*Penger*
Bottle	*Flaske*
Cocktail	*Cocktail*
Beer	*Øl*
Meat	*Kjøtt*
Fish	*Fisk*
Milk	*Melk*
Vegetables	*Grønnsaker*
Fruit	*Frukt*
Church	*Kirke*
Entrance	*Inngang*
Exit	*Utgang*
Folk Dances	*Folkedanser*

Ski	*Ski*
Skate	*Skøyte*
Sled	*Kjelke*
Spring	*Vår*
Summer	*Sommer*
Fall	*Høst*
Winter	*Vinter*
Sun	*Sol*
Moon	*Måne*
Star	*Stjerne*
Snow	*Snø*
Rain	*Regn*
Far	*Fjern*
Near	*När*
Music	*Musikk*
Shop	*Butikk*
Factory	*Fabrikk*
Hospital	*Sjukehus*
School	*Skole*
Post Office	*Postkontor*
Check	*Sjekk*
Airport	*Flyplass*
Railroad station	*Jernbanestasjon*
Mountain	*Fjell*
River	*Elv*
Lake	*Innsjø* or *vann*
Ocean	*Hav*
Sea	*Sjø* or *vann*
Walk	*Gå*
Wait	***Vente***
Bus	***Buss***
Road	***Veg***
Shore	*Strand*

APPENDIX D
A TALE OF ASKELADDEN

Once upon a time there was a very poor man who had three sons, Per, Pål and Espen Askeladd. He told them that they had better get out in the world and make their own living. If they stayed home they would surely starve to death.

Across the mountain the king had his big farm where a giant oak tree was shutting out the sunlight. Whenever somebody tried to cut it down it only grew bigger and thicker. The king also needed a well which could provide him with water all year round. All his neighbors had such wells, and the king felt it was a great shame that he was the only one without it. But the king's farm was way up on the mountain side and whenever they started to dig they found only hard rocks right away. The king announced that whoever could get rid of the oak tree for him and dig a deep enough well would get the princess in marriage and also half the kingdom.

Many tried but nobody succeeded. The oak grew bigger and bigger, and the rocks seemed to become harder and harder.

Per, Pål and Espen Askeladd also heard about the job and the reward and decided to try their luck. Their father liked the idea. Even if his sons would not win the princess and half the kingdom, they might join the king's service anyway and thus make a living.

The boys came to a tree-clad hill where they heard wood-chopping sounds.

"I wonder who is up there?" Espen Askeladd said.

"You and your wondering," his brothers replied. "What is so peculiar about wood-cutting in the forest?"

"Oh, I think I'll take a look anyway," Espen said. He climbed up the slope and found an axe chopping away at a tree.

"Good morning," said Espen Askeladd. "I see you are busy."

"Yes," replied the axe. "I have been waiting a long time for you."

Espen put the axe in his knapsack and went back to his brothers who laughed and teased him, asking if he had found anything.

"Only an axe," said Espen Askeladd.

The three brothers then came to a steep cliff where they

heard hammering and digging.

"I wonder what that can be?" said Espen Askeladd.

"You and your wondering," said Per and Pål. "What is so peculiar about hammering on stone?"

"Oh, I think I'll take a look anyway," said Espen Askeladd and climbed up on the cliff where he found a pick hammering and digging away.

"Good morning," said Espen Askeladd. "I see you are busy."

"Yes," replied the pick. "I have been waiting for you for a long time."

Espen put the pick in his knapsack and went back to his brothers who laughed harder than ever at him, asking if he had found anything.

"Only a pick," said Espen Askeladd.

Now they came to a brook and they were all three very thirsty.

"I wonder where all this water comes from?" said Espen Askeladd.

"We wonder if you are right in your head," his brothers jeered. "You and your wondering. Why don't you try to find out?"

"I sure will," Espen Askeladd replied and followed the brook upstream. It became smaller and smaller and finally he discovered a big walnut out of which the water flowed.

"Good morning," said Espen Askeladd. "I see you are busy."

"Yes," replied the walnut. I have been waiting for you for a very long time."

Espen put the walnut in his knapsack, but first he stuffed the hole with some pieces of moss to stop the water.

"Did you find out where the water came from?" his brothers laughed.

"Yes, from a hole," said Espen Askeladd who did not let it bother him that the brothers were making fun of him.

Finally they came to the king's farm, where the oak by now was twice as big as it had been when the king proclaimed the reward. The king was now so mad at all who had tried to cut it down that he had declared that all those who failed should have their ears cropped and be banished to an island.

Per and Pål were not afraid, however. They felt sure they could take care of the oak. Per tried first but for every limb he cut off two new ones grew on the tree. The king's men arrested him, cropped his ears and put him on the island. The same happened to Pål.

Then Espen Askeladd wanted to have his turn. The angry king said he might as well crop the boy's ears right away to save him the trouble with the tree and the well.

But Espen Askeladd insisted he try. He took his axe out of the knapsack. "Chop away!" he told the axe, and soon the tree was down. Then Espen took out the pick. "Dig away!" he told the pick. When the well was deep enough, Espen Askeladd took out his walnut, placed it in a corner of the bottom of the well, and removed the moss. "Fill the well!" he told the walnut, and soon the water was all the way up to the brim.

Espen Askeladd married the princess and got half the kingdom, and his brothers were better off without their ears; otherwise they would have been hearing all the time that it pays to wonder!

Snipp, snapp, snute, så er eventyret ute! (And that is the end of the fairy tale!)

APPENDIX E
NORWEGIAN MEASURES
Norwegian and the Corresponding American Sizes

MEN

Shirts

NOR.	AM.
36	14
37	14½
38	15
39	15½
40	15¾
41	16
42	16½
43	17
44	17½
45	18

Hats

NOR.	AM.
53	6⅝
54	6¾
55	6⅞
56	7
57	7⅛
58	7¼
59	7⅜
60	7½
61	7⅝
62	7¾

Coats, Overcoats, Pajamas

NOR.	AM.
44	34
46	36
48	38
50	40
52	42
54	44
56	46
58	48

Sweaters

NOR.	AM.
44	small
46-48	medium
50	large
52-54	extra large

Underwear

NOR.	AM.
5	small
6-7	medium
8	large
9-10	extra large

Shoes

NOR.	AM.
38-39	5-5½
39-40	6-6½
40-41	7-7½
41-42	8-8½
42-43	9-9½
43-44	10-10½
44-45	11-11½
45-46	12

Socks

NOR.	AM.
9	5½
9½	6½
10	7½
10½	8½
11	9½
11½	10½
12	11½
12½	12

LADIES

Young Ladies

NOR.	AM.
36	10
38	12
40	14
42	16
44	18
46	20

Ladies

NOR.	AM.
44	36
46	38
48	40
50	42
52	44

Junior Sizes

NOR.	AM.
36	9
38	11
40	13
42	15
44	17

Blouses

NOR.	AM.
38	32
40	34
42	36
44	38
46	40
48	42

Sweaters

NOR.	AM.
40	34
42	36
44	38
46	40
48	42
50	44

Stockings

NOR.	AM.
8½	8½
9	9
9½	9½
10	10
10½	10½
11	11

Shoes

NOR.	AM.
36-37	4½-5
37-38	5½-6
38-39	6½-7
39-40	7½-8
40-41	8½-9
41-42	9½-10
42-43	10½-11

APPENDIX F
PRIMARY SOURCES IN NORWAY FOR
GENEALOGICAL RESEARCH

If you require relatively recent information you should write directly to the authority concerned. The survey of sources given below will tell you which authority to approach. Should you still be in doubt, however, you can send your inquiry through a Norwegian Foreign Service Consulate or Embassy, and in that way it is also easier to arrange payment of fees (according to the official scale of charges). At most Norwegian Embassies and Consulates you will probably also be able to study *Norges Statskalender,* a book which lists the various government departments and other institutions and organizations (with addresses), their spheres of work and the names of all urban and rural districts. Also *Nordmanns-Forbundet* (The League of Norsemen), Rådhusgaten 23 B, Oslo, can advise you usefully about how to proceed in your quest.

What they can do is to supply certificates and copies—in some cases also photostats and film copies—according to a fixed scale of fees. They are also usually willing to put you in touch with a genealogist who will undertake research on your behalf and at your expense. If you visit Norway personally, you can study documents at the archives, and the staff will help and advise you. It is an advantage if you can read the old "Gothic" (German) style of lettering which was used in Norway until late in the 19th century.

There is one thing you should remember, whomever you approach, and that is: *Supply too much rather than too little information!*

Riksarkivet, the National Archives, preserves the non-current records of government departments and offices, while the various *statsarkivs* preserve documents from the regional and local branches of the State administration. No definite time limit is set for the transfer of records to the central archives. However, as far as the chief sources of genealogical information are concerned, you can generally expect that documents dating from before 1900 have been transferred.

Riksarkivet
Bankplassen 3, Oslo

If you know the name of the place in Norway your family

came from, you should approach the *statsarkiv* for that place. If you write to any archive you will usually receive some help.

For Counties of Østfold, Akershus, Oslo, Buskerud, Vestfold and Telemark:

> Statsarkivet i Oslo
> Kirkegaten 14-18, Oslo

For Counties of Hedmark and Oppland:

> Statsarkivet i Hamar
> Strandgaten 71, Hamar

For Counties of Aust-Agder and Vest-Agder:

> Statsarkivet i Kristiansand
> Vesterveien 4, Kristiansand

For Counties of Rogaland, Hordaland, Bergen and Sogn og Fjordane:

> Statsarkivet i Bergen
> Årstadveien 32, Bergen

For Counties of Møre og Romsdal, Sør-Trøndelag, Nord-Trøndelag, Nordland, Troms and Finnmark:

> Statsarkivet i Trondheim
> Høgskoleveien 12

PARISH REGISTERS (*Kirkebøker*)

These are records kept by the parish clergymen and give information about baptism, confirmation, marriage, and burial. Since the beginning of the 19th century they also record movements into and out of the parish. Some parish registers date from the 1600's but most are from after 1700. Not until about 1800 were parish registers given a standardized form. Registers less than about 80 years old are held by the parish clergymen; older registers are in the custody of the *statsarkivs*.

Registers less than 60 years old are not accessible to genealogical researchers without special permission.

Extracts from the parish registers since 1870 are held by *Statistisk Sentralbyrå* (Central Bureau of Statistics), Oslo. For the period 1866-69 extracts are deposited at *Riksarkivet*.

CENSUS RETURNS (*Folketellinger*)

Official census returns were made in 1769, 1801, and every tenth year from 1815 through 1875. Since 1890 also, a census of population has been taken every tenth year. All census returns from 1900 and earlier are available for in-

spection. They are all found at *Riksarkivet,* except for the
1875 and 1900 returns which are in the custody of the
statsarkivs.

The best from a genealogical point of view are the 1801
census, giving name, age, occupation, and family status, and
the census returns through 1865, which also give information
about each person s place of birth etc. The other census returns
give almost only statistical information. The 1769 census does,
however, provide some name lists, mostly from North Norway,
and the 1815-45 returns give lists of persons in a few scattered
parishes.

OLDER CENSUS RETURNS

Riksarkivet preserves a number of records predating the introduction of the national census. The most important are
the population rolls (*manntall*) 1664-66. These cover the
rural districts only and are entered in two parallel series, one
filled in by the parish clergymen, the other by the local law
officers. Apart from women engaged in farming, only men
(and boys over a certain age) are listed. The population roll
1701 lists only males in rural districts.

The *statsarkivs* also possess certain complete population records (for instance the so-called *sjeleregistre*—the "registries
of souls"), deposited partly in the ecclesiastical files, partly
in the civil files. In the *statsarkivs* you will also find copies of
some of the principal population records and census returns
relating to their particular districts (the originals are kept in
Riksarkivet).

PROBATE REGISTERS (*Skifteprotokoller*)

These show the registration, valuation, and division of real
estate and property of all kinds left by deceased persons and
give the names of heirs and guardians and much other family
information as well as much interesting data of an economic
and cultural nature. The oldest registers go back to about
1660. They were kept by the magistrate (*sorenskriver*) in the
rural districts and by the urban council clerk (*byskriver*) in
towns, and are now preserved in the *statsarkiv*. They are
usually quite voluminous and only some are indexed.
Riksarkivet preserves a number of special military probate
registers. There are also lists and extracts of the probate regis-

ters (*skiftedesignasjoner*) from about 1800 until 1850.

For genealogists the sources so far mentioned are the most important. As they are not concentrated in one place, you will have to "commute" between, for instance, *Riksarkivet* and the *statsarkivs* as and when your research makes progress. With some luck and a good deal of effort it is quite likely that you will be able to trace the main lines of your family. However, you must make use of other sources as well if you want to get more detailed information or if you are hunting for "missing links" or want to trace your ancestors still farther back in time.

COURT RECORDS

Court records are one of the sources you can go to if you want further information. Most of these records—the *tingbøker* in particular—are deposited at the *statsarkivs* but a few are found in *Riksarkivet*. They contain reports of civil and criminal actions, including so-called *odelssaker* (referring to allodial property rights), and sometimes you can find information here about entire families through several generations. Some go back to the early 17th century.

REGISTERS OF CONVEYANCES AND MORTGAGES
(*Skjøte- og pantebøker; panteregistre*)

These offer information about real estate conveyances, mortgages and other encumbrances on property, agreements and contracts, etc., often with much biographical material. They rarely go farther back than about 1720. Deeds from and after 1900 (but often from a later year) are held by the local magistrate or town council clerk (*sorenskriver* or *byskriver*). Earlier deeds are in the custody of the *statsarkivs*.

REAL ESTATE BOOKS

Real estate books called *matrikler* will give you the names of owners and cultivators of farms. The books from 1665 and 1723 (in *Riksarkivet*) are particularly important. More recent *matrikler* (from and after 1938) have been printed. There are quite a number of so-called *jordebøker,* to some extent with the same kind of information. The very oldest, from the middle ages, have been printed.

Various accounts also rank among the archive documents which you may find useful to consult. Most important are probably the county and bailiwick accounts (*lens* and *foge-*

dregnskaper) now deposited at *Riksarkivet*. These go back to the 16th century and include tax lists and real estate registers and other material which may help you trace the owners and cultivators of farms from year to year. Information of a more detailed character about individual persons is found in various supplementary tax rolls (*ekstraskatt-manntall*) of which the most important date from 1645, about 1647, 1710 ff., 1762 ff., and 1816 ff. The accounts of the bailiffs cover rural districts only, but there are also corresponding town accounts (*byregnskaper*).

The *statsarkivs* preserve numerous cash books in which magistrates have entered fees and other payments which people have made. A few cash books are also deposited at *Riksarkivet*.

In the town magistrate's archives (*magistratarkiv*) now in the custody of the *statsarkivs* are found, among other material, the citizenship registers (*borgerskapsprotokoller*). These tell you when a craftsman or merchant was given his civic rights. The oldest of the citizenship registers in a number of towns have been printed.

Registrations of civil marriages (permitted since 1845) are lodged at the office of the registrar (usually the notary public). The oldest registration records have been transferred to the *statsarkivs*.

EMIGRANT LISTS

Since the end of the 1860's the police in a number of districts have kept lists of emigrants with their name, home address, date of departure, destination, and name of ship.

These lists may often prove the best starting point for your inquiries.

They are kept at the local police station, but the oldest lists of Oslo, Kristiansand, and Bergen have been transferred to the *statsarkivs*. The *statsarkiv* in Oslo also has emigrant lists from the White Star Line's agent for the period 1883-1923. The Stavanger emigrant lists have been destroyed by fire.

All archives have a number of collections of genealogical and personal histories of various kinds in manuscript form, as well as a great many farm and family records, applications for official posts, and large quantities of individual letters. The oldest of these, the so-called diplomas often written on parchment, go far back into the middle ages and are the principal sources of information about that period. Most of them have been printed and published in *Diplomatarium Norwegicum* (19 volumes).

Collections such as the ones mentioned are also found in certain libraries, museums, and other institutions.

Institutions with photographic portrait collections of significance include *Universitetsbiblioteket,* Oslo; *Riksantikvariatet,* Kirkegaten 14-18, Oslo; and *Norsk Folkemuseum,* Bygdøy, Oslo.

The newspapers contain much personal and family information of a historical nature. Most newspapers are filed at *Universitetsbiblioteket,* Oslo.

You should note that the use of family coats of arms has been restricted to relatively few families, in particular the nobility, State officials, and the upper middle class. The so-called *bumerker,* used to mark tools and as signets and signatures, are not coats of arms. Their initials, however, can often help to solve genealogical problems.

POPULATION REGISTERS (*Folkeregistre*)

A register of population is now kept in all municipalities, but its usefulness is limited because it was first made compulsory in 1946. Before 1946 generally only the largest municipalities kept population registers and even the oldest of these go back only to the beginning of the present century.

The information given above is generally taken from a booklet entitled "How to trace your Ancestors in Norway," published by the Norwegian Government Foreign Service.